W9-CBC-233

PERSONAL FREEDOM & CIVIC DUTY ™

UNDERSTANDING YOUR
RIGHT TO FREE SPEECH

SALLY GANCHY AND
CLAUDIA ISLER

FREE SPEECH
4
STUDENTS

FREE SPEECH
4
STUDENTS

ROSEN
PUBLISHING®

New York

Published in 2012 by The Rosen Publishing Group, Inc.
29 East 21st Street, New York, NY 10010

First Edition

Library of Congress Cataloging-in-Publication Data

Ganchy, Sally.
Understanding your right to free speech/Sally Ganchy, Claudia Isler.
    p. cm. — (Personal freedom and civic duty)
Includes bibliographical references and index.
ISBN 978-1-4488-4667-2 (library binding)
1. Freedom of speech—United States—Juvenile literature. 2. United States. Constitution. 1st Amendment—Juvenile literature. I. Isler, Claudia II. Title.
JC591.G36 2012
323.44'30973—dc22

                                                    2010044134

Manufactured in the United States of America

CPSIA Compliance Information: Batch #S11YA: For further information, contact Rosen Publishing, New York, New York, at 1-800-237-9932.

On the cover: Students rally for free speech rights on the steps of the U.S. Supreme Court in Washington, D.C.

CONTENTS

INTRODUCTION

Americans frequently declare, "It's a free country. I can say what I want." But what do these words and this claimed freedom really mean? In which ways are Americans free to speak and act as they please?

For example, during the presidency of George W. Bush, many Americans expressed the belief that the president and his administration lied about Iraq having weapons of mass destruction in order to concoct a justification for invading that country. During the presidency of

Above: Members of the Black Tea Party burn a flag in Boston, Massachusetts. The group is opposed to both the Republican and the Democratic parties.

Barack Obama, many Americans expressed the belief that he wasn't really an American citizen and that his birth certificate was forged. Others openly stated that they hoped his domestic and foreign policies would fail. In both instances, many Americans felt that these attacks upon Presidents Bush and Obama amounted to treason. In the United States, treason is a serious charge: it means that an American citizen is attacking the United States and/or aiding the country's enemies. Anyone convicted of treason can receive a lifelong jail term or even a death sentence. So the question is: do Americans have the right to criticize their elected officials, or even the entire system of government, its agencies and policies, even if their speech might weaken the authority of the government and possibly the nation itself?

In 2010, the U.S. Army post Fort Bragg was the center of controversy when it hosted a Christian rock concert featuring faith-based inspirational speakers drawn from local Christian churches. Protesters argued that this violated the doctrine of separation of church and state and implied that the secular U.S. Army was publicly endorsing Christianity, making it a sort of state religion. Supporters and organizers of the concert countered that they were operating well within their constitutional rights—including freedom of religion and freedom of speech. So another question arises: do individuals, private organizations, and public entities have the right to talk about and/or endorse particular religious beliefs in public forums?

Also in 2010, would-be renters of units in an apartment complex on Staten Island, New York, began reporting that their applications had been denied based upon their age. All of the rejected applicants were retirees whose income was derived mostly from Social Security and pension payments, even though this income met the minimum requirements. Similarly, that same year, the Justice Department announced that the housing authority for the city of Royston, Georgia, had agreed to pay $270,000 to settle a lawsuit brought against it relating to how it awarded low-income housing units to applicants. Rather than awarding vacant housing units to whomever was next on the waiting list, the Royston Housing Authority steered applicants to units based on their race. African Americans, in particular, received less desirable housing at inferior rental terms and conditions. Both of these cases began with individual citizens expressing concern and outrage over apparently unfair and discriminatory practices, even in the face of potential legal counterattacks by the powerful private and public housing organizations. The question here is: do Americans have the right to call attention to unfair and discriminatory practices and make accusations of illegality against individuals, private corporations, and public governmental agencies?

Americans do indeed enjoy freedom of speech: the right to publicly express ideas and opinions, no matter how unpopular they might be. This right is protected by the Constitution. Written in 1787, the Constitution describes the principles that govern America. The Bill of Rights, which is the first ten amendments to the Constitution, was added in 1791 to describe the liberties that each citizen of the United States enjoys. These are rights that the government is sworn to protect, even when these individual and states' rights run counter to the federal government's interests. Each state in the Union also wrote its own constitution, and most of these state constitutions contain a bill of rights that guarantees freedom of expression.

The freedom of speech is enshrined in the Bill of Rights' very first amendment. At the same time, the Framers of the Constitution realized that there might need to be limits placed upon what people could say, especially in public. But they debated the question of what these limits would be. The Constitution is short, and its language is general, in part to avoid being too explicit and definitive about what is permitted or forbidden and to provide interpretive room for changing times and evolving social and political conditions, norms, and attitudes.

In every era of U.S. history, Americans have used their freedom of speech to protest injustices and propose new ways of thinking. For instance, in the nineteenth century and early twentieth century, suffragists Elizabeth Cady Stanton and Susan B. Anthony publicly demanded that American women obtain the right to vote. Similarly, the right to free speech enabled African American civil rights activists, including Martin Luther King Jr., to demand their rights as American citizens and to call for an end to racial inequality. Many people in the late 1960s and early 1970s used their right to free speech to protest the war in Vietnam.

The now widely accepted and supported messages of these reformers were not always welcomed by those in power or even by the majority of American citizens at the time. Luckily, their right to speak out was protected by the First Amendment. Today, people continue to struggle for the right to be heard. People also continue to fight for the right to read, discuss, listen to, watch, and think about whatever they choose, regardless of how popular or generally accepted the ideas behind it are.

When people talk about freedom of speech, they usually focus on the word "freedom," rather than "speech." Speech is an ambiguous concept. Every day, as new technologies develop, what we mean by "speech" expands. Originally, the First Amendment protected written, spoken, and printed words. Today, freedom of speech may also apply to radio and television broadcasts, movies, video games, and electronic or Web content, including text contained in blogs, chat rooms, Web sites, e-mail, and tweets.

New media beg the question: should any word, image, or act that has meaning be considered speech and therefore be protected under the First Amendment? Is speech limited to the idea being communicated, or does it also include the mode of communication? In other words, does the First Amendment protect everything that can be delivered and viewed via the Internet, television, and print newspapers, among other media? While some modes of communication are new and still emerging, the struggle to define the concept and nature of speech and to interpret the corresponding right to free speech has a long, complex, and contentious history. What follows is an examination and analysis of some of the most important, history-making precedents in several areas of First Amendment law, as well as some of the most compelling recent examples of landmark challenges to and defenses of free speech rights.

THE ORIGINS OF THE FIRST AMENDMENT

The Constitution of the United States and its first ten amendments, the Bill of Rights, were written by many of the same people who led the American Revolution (1775–1783). Their vision of a nation composed of free individuals served by a government of their own choosing, rather than ruled by tyrannical despots, was realized in the United States' earliest founding documents, including the Declaration of Independence, the Constitution, and the Bill of Rights.

The First Amendment of the Bill of Rights guarantees Americans' freedom of speech. It also guarantees the freedom of the press, freedom of religion, freedom of assembly, and freedom to petition the government with grievances. The individual's rights and freedoms would seem to take precedence over the exercise of government authority and intervention. Yet, as will be seen in this examination of free speech rights, there is a constant push-pull between the rights of the individual and the extent of government power to restrict certain forms of speech and expression.

THE DECLARATION OF INDEPENDENCE

In 1776, the Continental Congress appointed a committee to write what would become known as the Declaration of Independence. It was written by Thomas Jefferson and was called "The Unanimous Declaration of the Thirteen United States of America."

The Continental Congress understood that the document was not simply a statement of withdrawal from the British Empire; it was also a first step toward the creation of a guiding set of democratic principles for governing the new country. To that end, the Declaration speaks of the "inalienable rights" of men, stating "to secure these rights, governments are instituted among men, deriving their just powers from the consent of the governed." In other words, the government obtains its power from the people who choose it; it is not all-powerful in and of itself. The government does not grant rights—it exists to protect the rights that all people are born with and inherently possess. Among the rights the authors believed to be inalienable—unable to be denied a human being— were the right to free speech, the right to protest against the government, and the right to object to its policies.

THOMAS PAINE'S *COMMON SENSE*

This 1792 illustration depicts Thomas Paine holding a scroll containing his "Rights of Man" essay.

In the same year that the Declaration of Independence was written and circulated, the pamphlet *Common Sense* was also published. Its author, Thomas Paine, was a British citizen who moved to the American colonies in 1774. A political theorist and a writer, Paine produced a series of sixteen pamphlets during the American Revolution called The Crisis, of which *Common Sense* was one. *Common Sense* called for the American colonists to rebel against the British and to declare their independence from the crown.

The pamphlet, which was the first work to call publicly for the American colonies to separate from Britain, was wildly successful. It went through twenty-five editions in the first year after its publication. Paine's argument helped convince the majority of colonists that separation and rebellion were the only solutions to their disenchantment with British rule. His revolutionary views got him in legal trouble with British colonial officials, and he was forced to flee to France to escape imprisonment. Still, Paine had exercised his inalienable right to express his thoughts and opinions to the public, even if those ideas criticized the existing government or even advocated its overthrow.

CREATING THE U.S. CONSTITUTION

A governing document called the Articles of Confederation maintained order among the association of states during the Revolutionary War. But as the federation of colonies evolved into a young nation in the postrevolution years, its weaknesses soon became evident. The Articles of Confederation provided for no executive branch, including no president, and there was no federal judiciary. The states retained most governing powers. The federal government was so weak that it couldn't even impose and collect taxes, regulate foreign and domestic commerce and trade, or draft and fund a standing army and navy.

As a result, in mid-May 1787, a Constitutional Convention was convened. Fifty-five men representing all the states except Rhode Island met in Philadelphia, Pennsylvania, to debate and draft a document that set

Fireworks explode over Independence Hall in Philadelphia, Pennsylvania, where both the Declaration of Independence and the U.S. Constitution were drafted and adopted and where the Second Continental Congress met.

forth the principles that would guide the newly independent nation's government. It also outlined the form the national government would take. They called this document the Constitution. Specifically, the Constitution provided for more federal (as opposed to state) authority, especially over taxation, trade, and foreign commerce.

One group of men who attended the Constitutional Convention called themselves Federalists. The Federalists were a political party that believed in a strong federal government, endowed with many powers at the expense of state control and states' rights. They claimed that the states did not need to fear centralized authority as long as good people were in charge. Unfortunately, as products of the times in which they lived, these men lacked a more inclusive understanding of who was fit to lead. Their understanding of "good people" was limited to propertied, formally educated, white, Christian men like themselves.

The experiences of fighting a war and of struggling for survival as a young, inexperienced, and newly independent nation changed the political outlook of many Americans in the 1780s. At the outset of the war, most Americans believed the Jeffersonian notion "that government which governs best, governs least." By the late 1780s, however, many people had changed their minds and come to agree with the Federalists.

Federalists argued that the checks and balances among the legislative, executive, and judicial branches that would be created by the Constitution, along with the clear-cut division of state and national powers, would ensure that no one individual or party would be able to seize absolute control over the national government.

In contrast, Anti-Federalists at the Constitutional Convention wanted a weak central government, protection of individual and states' rights, and a loosely regulated economy. The Anti-Federalists insisted that the Constitution include a bill of rights that would spell out and protect individual and states' rights.

In the end, the Federalists won the battle for a strong federal government, and the Constitution was ratified in June 1788. Almost immediately, however, Anti-Federalists and much of the American public began campaigning for a bill of rights to be added to the Constitution. Congress member James Madison placed nineteen proposed amendments to the new Constitution before the House of Representatives. The states soon ratified ten of these, which officially became part of the Constitution on December 15, 1791.

The text of the First Amendment reads as follows: "Congress shall make no law respecting an establishment of religion, or prohibiting the free exercise thereof; or abridging the freedom of speech, or of the press; or the right of the people peaceably to assemble, and to petition the Government for a redress of grievances."

SAFEGUARDING THE CONSTITUTION AND ITS PROTECTIONS: THE FEDERAL JUDICIARY

After declaring the American colonies' independence from Britain, the Founding Fathers had to decide which form of government would best suit their new country. They wanted to create a system that would treat all citizens fairly, a system that would not be hijacked by a single ruler, party, or group.

After much debate and a failed first attempt at a Constitution—the short-lived Articles of Confederation—they decided to create a system of checks and balances, involving three branches of federal government. These are the executive branch (the president and his or her cabinet officers), the legislative branch (Congress, comprised of the House of Representatives and the Senate), and the judicial branch (the U.S. Supreme Court and lower federal courts). The Framers of the Constitution expected a democratically elected Congress and president to respect citizens' rights. But in case that failed, they provided for the courts to safeguard the liberties of individuals.

The federal court system is divided into three levels (and is separate from state courts that enforce state

A group portrait of the U.S. Supreme Court justices, including the newest justices Sonia Sotomayor *(top row, far left)* and Elena Kagan *(top row, far right)*. They are joined in the top row by Stephen Breyer and Samuel Alito, and in the bottom row by, from left to right, Clarence Thomas, Antonin Scalia, Chief Justice John Roberts, Anthony Kennedy, and Ruth Bader Ginsburg.

laws and judge alleged violations of those laws). The first level is federal district court, followed by the U.S. courts of appeals, and then the ultimate judicial authority in the country, the U.S. Supreme Court. The court system is organized hierarchically, in that higher courts can hear cases previously tried in lower courts and can either uphold or overturn a lower court's decision. The federal district court system has at least one bench or court in each state, as well as one in Washington, D.C., and one in Puerto Rico. Each district has from one to twenty judges, who are appointed by the president. Among other things, the district court oversees cases that involve violations of the Constitution or other federal laws.

The U.S. courts of appeals are superior to the district courts. Sometimes called the circuit courts, they consist of eleven judicial circuits throughout the states, with another in Washington, D.C. Depending on the circuit, these courts can be staffed with anywhere from six to twenty-seven judges. These courts hear appeals from the district courts and hear cases that challenge the orders of any federal agency. Since 1869, the Supreme Court has had one chief justice and eight associate justices. The Supreme Court has the final say on all cases that it hears. The Supreme Court reviews decisions made by the U.S. courts of appeals. It can even review the decisions made by state appeals courts, if the particular case involves a federal or constitutional issue.

UNDERSTANDING THE STATE COURT SYSTEM

The state court system is a lot more complicated than the federal one, and no two states employ exactly the same system. Like the federal system, the state court system is hierarchical. The lowest level of the state courts, known as the inferior courts, can include municipal courts, traffic courts, or justices of

THE NEW CONGRESS' MOST IMPORTANT LEGISLATION: RESTRICTING FREE SPEECH

Aside from the Bill of Rights, the most far-reaching piece of legislation enacted by the first Congress to operate under the new Constitution was a set of laws known as the Alien and Sedition Acts. In 1798, the Federalist-controlled Congress adopted these laws in an effort to suppress dissent and possible rebellion within the new nation. The Alien Acts affected foreign-born residents, or aliens, and provided for the detention of aliens from enemy countries in time of war. Further, it gave the president authority to deport anyone living in the country as an alien who seemed to threaten the nation. The fourth statute, the Sedition Act, sought to control both citizens and aliens. Generally, the act targeted sedition, or resistance to government authority. Specifically, it outlawed any conspiracies that sought to prevent the enforcement of federal laws, setting the maximum punishment for such offenses at five years in prison and a $5,000 fine.

The Sedition Act also tried to control speech. Writing, printing, or uttering "false, scandalous, and malicious" statements against the government or the president, "with the intent to defame...or to bring them or either of them, into contempt or disrepute" became a crime punishable by as much as two years imprisonment and a fine of $2,000. Today, any such law punishing speech alone would be considered unconstitutional. But in the eighteenth century, when a fledgling nation struggled to establish federal order and authority, organized political opposition became highly suspect. As a result, many Americans supported the Sedition Act's restriction on speech.

In response to these severe measures, in 1798 and 1799, the Kentucky and Virginia state legislatures passed resolutions contradicting the Alien and Sedition Acts. In fact, the Kentucky resolution stated that the government had no right to exercise powers not granted by the Constitution, and a state could undo federal laws if they were unfair. In the early years of the nineteenth century, the Alien Acts that unfairly targeted recently arrived immigrants expired or were repealed. Nevertheless, regulating sedition and the corresponding effects that such attempts at governmental control over ideas and opinions have on the right to free speech remained hotly debated issues throughout American history.

the peace. These courts hear only minor civil or criminal cases.

Superior courts, also known as state district courts or circuit courts, hear cases about more serious crimes, as well as appeals from inferior courts. Decisions in these courts are decided by jury. The highest state courts go by a variety of names: state supreme court, the appellate court, or state court of appeals. They hear appeals from the state superior courts and occasionally have original jurisdiction over very important cases. In between these three levels of state judiciary are a variety of other courts. The number of these courts varies from state to state.

SPEECH ACTS AND THE LIMITS OF FREE SPEECH

Scholars of the First Amendment have varying interpretations as to when and why speech warrants protection. Some constitutional experts interpret the right narrowly, arguing that the free speech clause of the First Amendment only protects the spoken word. Others believe in a broader understanding of the First Amendment, claiming that it also protects actions that express an opinion, or "speech acts." These advocates claim that the First Amendment protects freedom of expression and not simply freedom of speech.

Among more recent speech act controversies is flag burning. Historically, people have burned the American flag to protest government policies. To others, the flag is a sacred object that should never be burned. These people argue that burning a flag is an act (and a treasonous act at that), and not a form of speech, and should therefore not be protected by the First Amendment. The Supreme Court has ruled that flag burning is a form of symbolic speech. In 1989, the Supreme Court ruled in *Texas v.*

Johnson that this symbolic speech is protected under the First Amendment.

Other types of "free speech acts" and "symbolic speech" can include protest marches or sit-ins. The problem, some say, with considering certain actions free speech, lies in the regulation of those actions. As scholar Stanley Fish notes in Franklyn S. Haiman's *Speech Acts and the First Amendment*, "No one would think to frame a First Amendment that began 'Congress shall make no law abridging freedom of action'; for that would amount to saying 'Congress shall make no law,' which would amount to saying 'There shall be no law.'" Regulating what people do, not to mention what they say, is a tricky business, and Americans contradict themselves all the time when they argue about what is and isn't allowed under the First Amendment and the right to free speech that it protects. One Supreme Court case in particular examined the distinction between a free speech act and disorderly conduct.

DELIBERATE DEFIANCE

Irving Feiner, a college student in Syracuse, New York, was arrested on March 3, 1949, for breaking New York's disorderly conduct law. The law states:

> Any person who, with intent to provoke a breach of the peace: (1) uses offensive, disorderly,

threatening, abusive, or insulting language, conduct, or behavior; (2) acts in such a manner as to annoy, disturb, interfere with, obstruct, or be offensive to others; or (3) congregates with others on a public street and refuses to move on when ordered by the police; shall be deemed to have committed the offense of disorderly conduct.

Before his arrest, Feiner had stood on a box to address a racially diverse crowd of almost seventy-five people. The police who were called to the scene to investigate heard Feiner say, "The Negroes don't have equal rights; they should rise up in arms and fight for their rights," and "President Truman is a bum." The crowd began to react, some in favor of Feiner's ideas and some against them. There was some pushing and shoving. The police ordered Feiner to stop speaking because they thought he would start a riot. Feiner was arrested when he refused to end his speech. He was tried and convicted in the Syracuse City Court.

Feiner appealed his conviction in both the county and state courts of appeals, both of which upheld the verdict of the Syracuse City Court. So he appealed to the U.S. Supreme Court, arguing that his right to free speech had been violated under the Fourteenth Amendment. The Fourteenth Amendment protects all of the individual rights outlined in the Bill of Rights

An environmentalist is arrested outside the White House in Washington, D.C., during a protest against mountaintop-removal coal mining that opponents say results in water pollution and other environmental calamities.

by prohibiting individual states from denying those rights. If a state passes a law that limits free speech, the Fourteenth Amendment protects citizens from having to obey such a law.

The Supreme Court did not see it Feiner's way. He had been asked to come down off his box three times before he was arrested. The court believed that he had not been arrested for what he had said but for the potentially dangerous public disorder his words were causing. The crowd that had gathered while Feiner was speaking became angry, with one onlooker threatening violence if the police did not take action to stop Feiner. In addition, pedestrians were forced to walk in a street that was open to traffic to avoid the growing and jostling crowd on the sidewalk.

Chief Justice Fred Vinson delivered the verdict: "... the imminence of greater disorder, coupled with [Feiner's] deliberate defiance of the police officers, convinced us that we should not reverse this conviction in the name of free speech." According to the Supreme Court's decision, Feiner had not been arrested for suggesting that African Americans ought to fight for their rights, or for criticizing the president of the United States. He was arrested because he did not move when told to do so by the police, as the state's disorderly conduct law stipulates. He was also arrested for disturbing the peace because arguments were breaking out in the crowd that had gathered to hear him.

TESTING THE BOUNDARIES OF PUBLIC SPACE AND FREE SPEECH

While a significant percentage of Americans support at least some restrictions on speech, many others consider protecting free speech integral to preserving democracy in the United States. In order to protect freedom of speech, however, it's important to understand the limits of that freedom.

THE BOUNDARIES OF FREE SPEECH

Today, some Americans believe in strict limitations on free speech and speech acts. In their 2009 State of the First Amendment (SOFA) survey, the First Amendment Center found that 39 percent of Americans believed that the press has too much freedom. The 2008 SOFA survey found that 30 percent of those surveyed believed that people should not be allowed to say things that might be offensive to a religious group in public, while 42 percent believed that people should be prohibited from publicly saying things that might offend other racial groups. Thirty-three percent of those surveyed believed that school officials should be given the power to punish students who posted material that the school didn't like online, even when that material was posted outside school, on home computers, after school hours.

Americans can exercise their freedom of speech to some degree in some, but not all, public spaces. A person may exercise his or her right to free speech in public places, such as parks and streets. Such places are called public forums. Not all public spaces qualify, however. For instance, people may not begin political rallies in the post office or in the welfare office. The government may also regulate the time at which demonstrations occur and the way in which citizens come together and use public space.

A street protester in New York City's Times Square warns passersby that "the end is near" on the eve of New Year's celebrations.

One group that has been instrumental in testing and defining the limits of the First Amendment is the American Civil Liberties Union (ACLU), a nonpartisan organization that was established in 1920. Its goal is to protect the rights guaranteed to Americans by the Constitution. In particular, it focuses on freedom of expression and equality before the law. The ACLU has a very large membership and has been involved in nearly every important civil liberties case since its inception. According to the ACLU, the First Amendment protects speech, no matter how offensive it is. In a summary of the organization's goals and policies, the ACLU states, "How much we value the right of free speech is put to its severest test when the speaker is someone we disagree with most."

Americans continue to struggle to define the limits of free speech. Should individual speech be protected even if it endangers the country? Is the nation's security so important that it automatically gives the government the right to infringe upon, curtail, or even deny outright individual rights? These questions have been urgently asked throughout the history of the United States, and the answers, such as they are, have varied depending on the circumstances and the times.

FREE SPEECH
DURING WARTIME

World War I broke out more than one hundred years after the Framers of the Constitution had guaranteed the right to free speech in the First Amendment. The Great War, as it was known, lasted from 1914 to 1918. During wartime, many wondered: do Americans have the right to voice their disagreement with government policy, especially at a time of national crisis?

World War I was fought in Europe between the Allies (France, Great Britain, Russia, and the United States) and the Central Powers (Germany, Austria-Hungary, and Turkey). It was one of the bloodiest wars in history: Sixty-five million men and women served in the military, and about ten million people were killed. Twice that number were wounded. Naturally, these numbers upset many Americans and fueled anti-war sentiment in the United States.

Initially, President Woodrow Wilson had promised to keep the United States out of the war. In 1915, however, German U-boats attacked and sank the British passenger ship *Lusitania*; Americans on board were killed, and, as a result, President Wilson found it impossible to remain neutral. In April 1916, Wilson asked Congress to approve a declaration of war. The United States was divided not only between people against American participation in the war and those for it, but also along ethnic lines. One of every three Americans was either foreign-born or the child of a foreign-born parent. Many of the thirty-two million Americans with strong family ties to foreign nations came from countries that were now considered enemies, such as Germany and Austria-Hungary. Wilson believed he needed to develop a way to unify the American people against the Central Powers and get them behind the war effort. One method he devised was the Committee on Public Information (CPI).

PROPAGANDA AND CENSORSHIP DURING WORLD WAR I

Formed in 1917, the Committee on Public Information endeavored to convince the public to support the war effort enthusiastically. Simply put, the CPI wanted to sell the war to Americans. To that end, it implemented an enormous propaganda campaign. Propaganda is information, often incomplete, erroneous, or overly slanted, that is disseminated in order to influence the way people think. The CPI hired approximately seventy-five thousand speakers, known as

This 1917 poster produced by the Committee on Public Information's Four-Minute Men movement presented its pro-war message within the urgent and patriotic context of the Revolutionary War, including images of town criers and Independence Hall.

"Four-Minute Men," who gave moving, patriotic speeches in schools, churches, movie theaters, and other public places. It distributed millions of pamphlets in a number of languages that explained America's role in the war. The CPI even produced pro-involvement, anti-Central Powers movies, including *Kaiser, The Beast of Berlin.* Kaiser was the official title of the ruler of Germany. Another film, *To Hell with the Kaiser,* was so popular that Massachusetts riot police were called in to calm an angry mob that had been turned away at an overcrowded theater.

The committee also engaged in censorship of allegedly dangerous information. This means that its agents combed through books and newspapers

JEANNETTE RANKIN (1880–1973), PACIFIST HEROINE

Jeannette Rankin was a suffragist and a pacifist. She was also the first woman elected to Congress, serving two terms in the House of Representatives, the first beginning in 1917, and the second in 1941. In 1917, only a month after she took her seat in Congress representing the state of Montana, she was one of fifty House representatives who voted against declaring war on Germany, saying, "I want to stand by my country, but I cannot vote for war." She paid a heavy price for her refusal to compromise her pacifist ideals—the press attacked her, and even her fellow suffragettes distanced themselves from her. She also voted against the Espionage Act of 1917.

But despite the backlash against Rankin's actions, she never stopped working for peace. In the 1920s, she was an officer of the Women's International League for Peace and Freedom, and she served as a lobbyist for the Women's Peace Union, where she campaigned to outlaw war. In 1929, she joined the National Council for the Prevention of War. In 1941, she cast the only vote against the declaration of war on Japan, and, in 1968, she led a group of about five thousand people to Washington, D.C., in order to demonstrate against the Vietnam War.

looking for information or opinions they thought could damage the war effort and suppressed them so that they never reached the wider public. Journalists were given official guidelines regarding what they could say and write. The CPI urged neighbors to spy on neighbors and to report any supposedly disloyal feelings they sensed or unpatriotic sentiments or actions they overheard or observed. Business owners and managers were encouraged to spy on their employees. Not surprisingly, an atmosphere of deep mistrust quickly enveloped the entire country.

Legislating Conformity: The Espionage Act of 1917 and the Sedition Act of 1918

During World War I and under President Woodrow Wilson, the American government became obsessed with silencing dissenting political opinion. Congress passed the Espionage Act in 1917, which was amended by the Sedition Act in 1918. The Sedition Act made it illegal to criticize the war or the government in any way. German Americans could not voice worries about their homeland or relatives, nor could any American citizen say out loud, in public, "We should not be at war." Playing German music and teaching or speaking the German language was prohibited. In everyday conversation, familiar German words were replaced, so that "sauerkraut" became "liberty cabbage" or "victory cabbage." Songs such as "Oh, Tannenbaum" ("Oh, Christmas Tree") were torn out of books of Christmas carols. Towns changed German street names. German Americans were often

A mock funeral is held for the "Beast of Berlin," Kaiser Wilhelm II, in this World War I–era American photograph. Anti-German sentiment ran high during the war, and anyone who opposed American involvement in it risked being labeled a traitor or German sympathizer.

pressured to change their names, lost their jobs, and in a few cases, were even beaten or murdered.

Many Americans had good reason to oppose World War I, but citizens were banned from speaking their minds. It was only a matter of time before the issue of political censorship came before the Supreme Court.

"CLEAR AND PRESENT DANGER"

Charles Schenck was the general secretary of the U.S. Socialist Party. The party's main office was in

Philadelphia, Pennsylvania. The party campaigned against American involvement in World War I and against drafting people to fight it. In 1917, under Schenck's direction, the group hoped to send out letters to fifteen thousand draft-age men. The letters argued that conscription, or the draft, was despotic and thus urged the men to resist the call to arms. In fact, the letters stated that it was the men's civic and patriotic duty to resist the draft and thereby stand up for their constitutional civil rights and those of all Americans.

The police raided the Socialist Party's headquarters, seized all its mailings, and arrested Schenck. He was accused of violating the Espionage Act by passing out antiwar literature. In federal district court, he was tried for conspiracy to violate the Espionage Act. Schenck argued that his First Amendment right of free speech rendered the Espionage Act unconstitutional. Nevertheless, Schenck was convicted. He appealed his conviction to the U.S. Supreme Court. Justice Oliver Wendell Holmes explained the decision of the Court:

> ...the character of every act depends upon the circumstances in which it is done. The most stringent protection of free speech would not protect a man in falsely shouting "fire" in a theater, and causing a panic...The question in every case is whether the words used are used in such circumstances and are of such a nature as to

THE SEDITION ACT OF 1918

Section three of the Sedition Act of 1918 states:

Whoever, when the United States is at war, shall willfully make or convey false reports or false statements with intent to interfere with the operation or success of the military or naval forces of the United States, or to promote the success of its enemies, or shall willfully make or convey false reports, or false statements...or incite insubordination [disobedience], disloyalty, mutiny [rebellion], or refusal of duty, in the military or naval forces of the United States, or shall willfully obstruct...the recruiting or enlistment service of the United Stales, or...shall willfully utter, print, write, or publish any disloyal, profane, scurrilous, or abusive language about the form of government of the United States...or shall willfully display the flag of any foreign enemy, or shall willfully...urge, incite, or advocate any curtailment [reduction] of production...or advocate, teach, defend, or suggest the doing of any of the acts or things in this section enumerated [listed], and whoever shall by word or act oppose the cause of the United States therein, shall be punished by a fine of not more than $10,000 or imprisonment for not more than twenty years, or both...

create a clear and present danger that they will bring about substantive evils that Congress has a right to prevent...When a nation is at war, many things that might be said in time of peace are such a hindrance to its effort that their utterance will not be endured so long as men fight, and that no court could regard them as protected by any constitutional right.

The Supreme Court had concluded unanimously that war was a special circumstance in which Americans could not say whatever they liked about the government.

"EVERY IDEA IS AN INCITEMENT"

Passed in 1902, New York State's Criminal Anarchy Law stated that it was a crime to try to encourage the violent overthrow of the government. Benjamin Gitlow was a member of the Socialist Party during the 1920s. In 1923, he published and circulated sixteen thousand copies of the *Left-Wing Manifesto*. The pamphlet supported the creation of a socialist system in the United States through massive strikes and "class action...in any form." Gitlow was arrested for circulating these pamphlets and promoting political agitation through his writings. He was tried and convicted in the New York State Supreme Court, but he appealed to the U.S. Supreme Court, arguing that his First Amendment right to freedom of speech (and of the press) had been violated.

The Supreme Court ruled in favor of Gitlow. In its decision, delivered by Justice Holmes, the Court stated

Benjamin Gitlow, a prominent socialist and founding member of the Communist Party USA, testifies before Congress in 1939.

that "...for present purposes, we may assume that freedom of speech and of press...are among the fundamental personal rights and liberties protected by the due process clause of the Fourteenth Amendment from impairment by the State." Justice Holmes continued:

> It is said that [Gitlow's] manifesto was more than a theory, that it was an incitement. Every idea is an incitement. It offers itself for belief, and, if believed, it is acted on unless some other

belief outweighs it or some failure of energy stifles the movement at its birth. The only difference between the expression of an opinion and an incitement in the narrower sense is the speaker's enthusiasm for the result.

Gitlow was accused on the grounds of trying to violently overthrow the government. The Court realized that the publishing and distribution of pamphlets did not constitute violent overthrow. Consequently, the Court concluded that Gitlow's arrest violated his First Amendment right to free speech and freedom of the press, and his Fourteenth Amendment right to due process.

Justice Holmes argued that Gitlow's expression of his opinions and political theories was not only protected speech but also no more unsettling to the state or its citizens than any expression of an idea. The test of an idea's validity or invalidity is whether someone believes it, acts upon it, and continues to believe in its validity after seeing how it works in practice. Bad or dangerous ideas tend to have short lives and few believers, and therefore government does not need to artificially extend the life of bad or dangerous ideas by trying to suppress them. Common sense and pragmatism offer the best protection against objectionable or misguided ideas, Holmes believed, not government censorship.

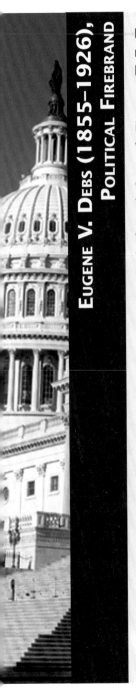

EUGENE V. DEBS (1855–1926), POLITICAL FIREBRAND

Eugene Debs was a political activist who organized the American Railway Union in 1892. He helped found the Social Democratic Party in 1897, which was renamed the Socialist Party in 1901. He ran for president of the United States in 1900, 1904, 1908, and 1912. In 1912, Debs won 6 percent of the national vote.

On June 16, 1918, Debs enthusiastically delivered a speech in Canton, Ohio, extolling the virtues of socialism and freedom of speech. He also argued for the right to criticize the Wilson administration for taking America into World War I. Debs urged his audience to resist the World War I draft. Soon afterward, he was arrested and charged with sedition. The court ruled against Debs, sentencing him to ten years in prison. Upon hearing his sentence, Debs told the court that the Espionage Act was a tyrannical, anti-democratic law that violated the very spirit of American freedom and liberty.

Debs appealed his conviction, taking his case all the way to the Supreme Court. However, in *Debs v. United States*, the Court found that Debs had indeed obstructed the draft, so his conviction had to stand under the precedent set by *Schenck v. United States*. Debs remained in prison until late 1921, when he received a pardon.

In arriving at this decision, Justice Holmes asked a question that is still relevant today: if we do not tolerate others' opinions, how can we insist upon the right to speak our own minds? How can we expect our freedom of speech to be respected and protected if we suppress speech that we don't agree with? Holmes argued that to preserve freedom in the United States, the court should preserve Americans' freedom to debate the issues vital to their nation.

9/11, the PATRIOT Act, and Free Speech

In the wake of the terrorist attacks of September 11, 2001, the U.S. government, under President George W. Bush, gained new powers to monitor the activities and communications of its citizens, including the ability to listen in on phone conversations, monitor private e-mail and other Internet activity, and even track library loans and bookstore purchases. This was largely achieved through the passage of the USA PATRIOT Act. The government retained and continued to use these powers under the succeeding administration of President Barack Obama.

In the name of protecting Americans from possible terrorist plots brewing in their midst, the government was also viewed by some as using its new surveillance powers to quash dissent for its policies, particularly its

A man protests the USA PATRIOT Act during the Democratic National Convention in Boston, Massachusetts. The PATRIOT Act was viewed by many as overreaching in its efforts to protect national security and thereby trampling upon civil liberties and citizens' rights to privacy.

foreign and military policies in Iraq and Afghanistan. Some colleges and universities began to report that military intelligence agents and federal judges demanded information and records, including lists of attendees, for various antiwar or Islamic-themed conferences held on campus. The U.S. Senate considered a bill that would allow the national security agencies to oversee universities' curricula, course materials, reading lists, and hiring decisions.

Perhaps most disturbingly, the prospects for an open, honest, and vigorous debate on the effects of the so-called War on Terror on American civil liberties and the validity of the justification for the war in Iraq that soon followed 9/11 were greatly dampened when the attorney general at the time, John Ashcroft, said that critics of the Bush administration's efforts were giving "aid and comfort to the enemy." Ashcroft was essentially accusing all those who disagreed with the Bush administration's policies of not only a lack of patriotism but also, far more gravely, of treason.

The PATRIOT Act, the War on Terror, and the war efforts in Iraq and Afghanistan seemed to have a chilling impact on American civil liberties, particularly on free speech and the right to express dissent with one's government.

CHAPTER 4

Like the early twentieth century and the turbulent World War I years, the 1960s were a time of enormous social upheaval and transformation. In response to official and unofficial forms of racial segregation in the United States and to a history of being denied their full rights as American citizens, many African Americans began to organize peaceful protests, marches, and sit-ins. They formed the vanguard of the civil rights movement. Eventually Americans of all racial and ethnic backgrounds who decided they could no longer tolerate segregation and racism banded together. Their brave and stubborn use of free speech and symbolic speech actions to protest an unjust American society led directly to profound changes in U.S. law, government, business, education, culture, and daily life.

THE MONTGOMERY BUS BOYCOTT

One of the most important events of the civil rights movement was the Montgomery

A poster on a New York City bus commemorates the fiftieth anniversary of Rosa Parks' act of civil disobedience that launched the Montgomery bus boycott in 1955, in which segregation on public transportation and other issues of racial discrimination were protested.

bus boycott. A boycott is a refusal to buy goods or services or to participate in an activity in order to protest a government's or company's decision or policy. Until 1955, African Americans were allowed to sit only in the back of city buses in Montgomery, Alabama, and were required to give up their seats to white passengers if the bus became crowded.

On December 1, 1955, Rosa Parks, an African American woman, refused to give up her seat to a white man and was arrested. Her arrest inspired a boycott: members of the African American community decided they would no longer ride city buses until they were treated fairly. This boycott was a free speech act. It was a physical and economic demonstration of how African Americans felt about segregation.

In 1956, the Supreme Court ruled in *Gayle v. Browder* that segregation on buses was unconstitutional. By making their voices heard, African Americans had captured an important victory. It took time for governmental authorities to successfully implement the Court's ruling, though. Initially, angry whites shot at some city buses and their African American passengers, causing the suspension of bus service until the violence stopped.

SITTING DOWN FOR CIVIL RIGHTS

Another form of nonviolent protest is a sit-in. This is a speech action in which protesters occupy and sit down in a place and refuse to move until a policy is changed. During the civil rights movement, one of the first sit-ins took place in Greensboro, North Carolina, in 1960. Four African American college students bought some school supplies at Woolworth's (a nationwide five-and-dime store, now out of business) and then sat down at the store's whites-only lunch counter. They had not been given service by the time the store closed, so they went home.

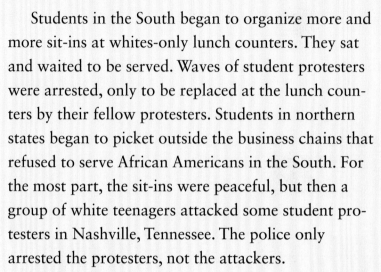

Students in the South began to organize more and more sit-ins at whites-only lunch counters. They sat and waited to be served. Waves of student protesters were arrested, only to be replaced at the lunch counters by their fellow protesters. Students in northern states began to picket outside the business chains that refused to serve African Americans in the South. For the most part, the sit-ins were peaceful, but then a group of white teenagers attacked some student protesters in Nashville, Tennessee. The police only arrested the protesters, not the attackers.

Sit-ins continued into the following year. Finally, in 1964, the Civil Rights Act was passed. It gave the U.S. attorney general more power to protect American citizens against discrimination and segregation in voting, education, and the use of public facilities. Once again, ordinary American citizens taking advantage of their First Amendment rights had changed the country.

"Don't Move"

During the civil rights era, there were countless demonstrations protesting racist public, educational, business, and governmental policies. In Baton Rouge, Louisiana, twenty-three civil rights protesters, all students at Southern University, were arrested on December 14, 1961. They had been picketing outside stores with segregated lunch counters. On December 15, two thousand more protesters marched to the

In 1960, African Americans engage in a sit-down demonstration, or sit-in, at a lunch counter that refused to serve them.

Baton Rouge courthouse to demonstrate their objection to these arrests. The chief of police asked them twice to disband as they readied for their march. Reverend B. Elton Cox, field secretary of the Congress of Racial Equality, or CORE, led the march.

When the group arrived at the courthouse, Cox was instructed by the chief of police to keep the demonstration on the west side of the street (across the street from the courthouse), which he did. There was a small crowd, mostly of curious courthouse personnel, gathered on the east side of the street, and there were about seventy-five police officers as well as members of the fire department stationed between the two groups. The protesters carried signs that named certain businesses whose practices were unfair. Standing five people deep on the sidewalk outside the courthouse, the demonstrators recited the Lord's Prayer, sang "God Bless America" and "We Shall Overcome," listened to a speech by Cox, and cheered him on. When they heard the twenty-three jailed protesters singing, too, they cheered and applauded loudly.

As Cox's speech concluded, he instructed the crowd to head for sit-ins at the nearby lunch counters. He said these stores were open to the public, and the African American protesters were all tax-paying members of the public and therefore had a right to be served lunch just like the white customers. The sheriff thought this speech was inflammatory, so he took the microphone from Cox and told the crowd to disperse. Some say Cox told his followers, "Don't move," and others say he made a gesture of defiance. The crowd did not disperse. When the police fired tear gas at them, the protesters ran.

On December 16, Reverend Cox was arrested and later convicted for blocking public sidewalks, disturbing the peace, and picketing before a courthouse. An additional charge of conspiracy was dropped. On appeal, the state supreme court upheld the conviction. Cox then appealed his case to the U.S. Supreme Court, arguing that his conviction for a street protest was a violation of the First Amendment. The Supreme Court agreed with Cox, stating that the cheering, clapping, and singing of the protesters did not constitute a disturbing of the peace or "fighting words." The gathering itself was not found to be inherently dangerous.

In fact, the protest had been peaceful. Reporters had captured it on film, so the Court had plenty of opportunities to observe that Cox had only exercised his constitutional rights. The Court also reversed the conviction of Cox under the "obstructing public passages" statute, showing that Baton Rouge's practices for regulating parades and meetings were unconstitutional. The officials in charge of such permits had been picking and choosing whose voices could be heard in the streets of Baton Rouge and whose could not.

Protesting the Vietnam War

The civil rights movement had taught many Americans the power of speaking out for what they believed in. The victories of this era proved that outspoken voices could change the world. Indeed, many people would soon invoke the lessons of the civil rights movement in their protest against the deepening war in Vietnam.

Vietnam, a country in Southeast Asia, has a long history of conflict with its neighbors—Thailand, Cambodia, Laos, and China. In 1954, the country was divided in two: Communist North Vietnam and the American-backed Nationalist South Vietnam. War broke out in South Vietnam as guerrillas led by the Communists, called the Viet Cong, tried to overthrow the South Vietnamese government.

As early as 1961, the United States began supplying troops to support South Vietnam. In 1964, after the North Vietnamese allegedly attacked an American destroyer, Congress gave President Lyndon Johnson the power to send as many troops to Vietnam as he saw fit. In 1965, U.S. forces began a massive bombing campaign against North Vietnam. The war effort expanded rapidly. By 1969, there were approximately 550,000 American troops in Vietnam, fighting a war

Vietnam-era antiwar protesters are confronted by military police during a 1967 rally outside the Pentagon in Arlington, Virginia.

on foreign and unfamiliar terrain—the dense jungle. At home, false official reports that the war was going well were soon discredited by independent journalism.

As the fighting in Vietnam unfolded, more and more Americans began to question the government's decision to send troops there. Young people began to demand answers. They wanted to know why the scheduled peace talks consistently failed and sought to understand why the troops were fighting. On many occasions, government reports about events in Vietnam were shown to be far from truthful. Also, news coverage revealed the gruesome and violent reality of war to Americans on a daily basis. In the meantime, more and more American soldiers died.

President Johnson also instituted the military draft. Registering with the Selective Service is a part of the draft process. The Selective Service is mandatory service in the U.S. armed forces. When young men turn eighteen, they are required to register with the Selective Service. During the Vietnam War, registering was likely to result in being drafted, or placed in military service. Some men went willingly. Some were forced to go, whether they wanted to or not.

Students on college campuses, who were exempt from the draft because of their status as students, began to organize antiwar protests and events. Political organizations such as Students for a Democratic Society (SDS) held rallies and organized marches. Rallies, marches, protests, demonstrations, and sit-ins were taking place all over the country. Some of these protests turned violent.

THE KENT STATE MASSACRE

On May 1, 1970, hundreds of angry antiwar students from Kent State University descended on downtown Kent, causing $5,000 worth of property damage. On May 3, Ohio governor James Rhodes arrived at Kent State, where he called the students the worst type of people in America and promised to "eradicate the problem." The atmosphere on campus became even more tense and confrontational. That same day, Ohio National Guardsmen attacked students with tear gas, rifles, and bayonets, injuring some. By May 4, hundreds of National Guardsmen had been stationed on the Kent State campus, in advance of a planned peaceful antiwar rally.

As the rally began, Guardsmen fired tear gas at the student protesters. Chaos erupted as they chased fleeing students. Rocks began to be thrown from both sides. Some students approached the Guardsmen aggressively, shouting at them. The Guardsmen retreated up a hill. Some of them then began shooting live ammunition for a sustained period at the students. Four students were killed, and nine were injured.

Two of the students killed, Allison Krause and Jeff Miller, were protesters. Sandy Scheuer and Bill Schroeder were innocent onlookers. None of the Guardsmen were ever convicted in these assaults and deaths. The National Guard, a military branch of both the federal and state governments, violently suppressed the Kent State protesters' exercise of free speech, and the government did not see fit to punish anyone for this extreme and deadly violation of American citizens' constitutional rights.

THE BERRIGAN BROTHERS, PRIESTS AND PROTESTERS

Daniel and Philip Berrigan were brothers, both Catholic priests, both activists. They garnered national attention when together they destroyed Vietnam War draft records and registration files in Catonsville, Maryland. They were each sentenced to three years in prison for this act. Although this was a speech act, it also destroyed government property and impeded the draft. The Berrigan brothers went into hiding to avoid imprisonment. They were eventually caught and served some time in prison. This was only one of the many times in the brothers' lives that they were arrested for acts protesting government policies.

The Berrigans devoted their lives to peace. Daniel went to Hanoi, North Vietnam, to help win the release of three American pilots in 1968. He is also a poet and has written more than fifty books, including *Night Flight to Hanoi*. Philip, who died in 2002, spoke out against the arms race and nuclear weapons proliferation. He was a founding member of the Ploughshares group, which organizes nonviolent and direct actions against nuclear weapons manufacturers.

INSIDE THE SCHOOLHOUSE GATE

In 1969, a case concerning one young person's right to free speech reached the Supreme Court. A few years earlier, on December 16, 1965, eighth-grader Mary Beth Tinker wore a black armband to Warren Harding Junior High School in Des Moines, Iowa, to express her opposition to the war in Vietnam. She attended her morning classes and went to lunch. After lunch, on her way to algebra class, she was called to the principal's office.

Principal Chester Pratt told Mary to take off her armband; she did. He then suspended her and sent her home. The Des Moines school board had ordered that no one could wear armbands to school, as they posed a threat to the peaceful operation of schools and administrative control over students.

Meanwhile, at Des Moines' Roosevelt High School, tenth-grader Chris Eckhardt was also suspended for wearing a black armband. Mary Tinker's father, a Methodist minister, called a meeting of students and parents to discuss the armband issue. They issued a statement indicating that the school board's denial of their children's opportunity to engage in this form of expression concerned them. Students had asked the school board to call an emergency meeting to discuss the ban, but the school board president argued that the issue was not important enough to warrant deviating from the meeting schedule.

By the next day, three more Des Moines students had been suspended, including Mary's brother, John, a tenth-grader at North High School. Interestingly, at these very same schools, students had been allowed to wear buttons in support of a variety of political campaigns. Some students were even allowed to wear the Iron Cross, a Nazi symbol.

The Des Moines school board met and, after much heated debate, voted to keep the ban on armbands in place. The controversy did not end there, however. The Iowa Civil Liberties Union (ICLU), a state branch of the national ACLU, brought a suit against the Des Moines school board in federal court, seeking to lift the ban. But the judge considered the school board's policy reasonable, stating that although the students wearing armbands were peaceful and there had been no evidence or complaint of any actual disturbance, the potential existed for disturbances in reaction to the armbands. The board argued that these reactions might disrupt regular school operations.

Still unsatisfied, the Tinkers took the case to the Supreme Court, where it was heard in November 1968. The case did not begin well; Justice Hugo Black had misunderstood the circumstances and had assumed that Mary had disrupted her algebra class. Allan Herrick, a lawyer representing the school board, tried to link Mary and the other suspended students with Students for a Democratic Society (SDS), pointing out that Chris and his mother had participated in an SDS-sponsored demonstration in Washington, D.C. In the end, Mary Beth Tinker won. This case was an important victory for advocates of free speech and free expression advocates, especially for the First

Amendment rights of minors. Justice Abe Fortas delivered the Court's decision:

> [The wearing of armbands] was closely akin to "pure speech," which, we have repeatedly held, is entitled to comprehensive protection under the First Amendment...It can hardly be argued that either students or teachers shed their constitutional rights to freedom of speech or expression at the schoolhouse gate...Any variation from the majority's opinion may inspire fear. Any word spoken, in class, in the lunchroom, or on the campus, that deviates from the views of another person may start an argument or cause a disturbance. But our Constitution says we must take this risk.

Like Mary Beth Tinker, many Americans expressed themselves in both word and deed during the civil rights movement and the years of the Vietnam War. They risked arrest and imprisonment, beatings, and even murder, placing their trust in the Constitution's assurance that "Congress shall make no law...abridging the freedom of speech."

UNWANTED SPEECH

Two decades after the heyday of the civil rights and antiwar movements, conservative and liberal protesters alike continued to employ highly visible and effective ways of communicating their political opinions to a broad audience.

In May 1985, the town of Brookfield, Wisconsin, passed an antipicketing ordinance that placed a total ban on residential picketing. Community leaders developed the ordinance in response to a group of antiabortion protesters who had picketed directly outside the home of Dr. Benjamin Victoria, a local doctor who performed abortions in a few nearby clinics. The group had picketed his house at least six times in the two months before the ordinance was passed.

Sandra Schultz was one of the picketers. When she realized that further picketing outside Victoria's house would end in her arrest, Schultz went to federal district court to sue Town Supervisor Russell Frisby. Schultz argued that the antipicketing ordinance was a violation of her First Amendment right to free speech. The ordinance was struck down by the district court, a verdict supported by the federal court of appeals, which called the town law "repugnant to the Constitution." On the surface, these courts appear to be correct. Schultz and her fellow protesters were exercising their right to free speech and their right to freedom of assembly, which gives Americans the freedom to come together in protest. The town of Brookfield then appealed the lower court's decision to the Supreme Court.

ANTIWAR T-SHIRTS: UNPOPULAR, OFFENSIVE, BUT PROTECTED

In 2010, a federal court in Tennessee dismissed a lawsuit brought against Dan Frazier, a peace activist who sells antiwar T-shirts over the Internet. His shirts featured the names of the more than four thousand servicemen and women killed in Iraq. Over these names appear the words, "Bush Lied...They Died." A portion of the proceeds from these T-shirt sales are donated to families of deceased soldiers. Yet one family of a soldier killed in the line of duty sued Frazier, who was represented in court by the Tennessee chapter of the ACLU.

Judge Ronnie Greer wrote in his decision, "The defendants are correct that exercising free speech in criticizing the government is not outrageous...The views expressed by the defendants may be unpopular and even offensive to some people, but they do not rise to the level of legal outrageous conduct" (as quoted by an American Civil Liberties Union press release). The court found that Frazier's T-shirts were a form of political speech, which is protected by the First Amendment, and that Frazier did not use soldiers' names to endorse or encourage others to buy the shirts, but "to make a political statement, which is an exercise of free speech."

Patricia Herzfeld, a staff attorney with the Tennessee branch of the ACLU, was quoted as saying, "Our sympathy goes out to the families of fallen soldiers. But this case goes beyond this particular shirt to the larger issue of chilling protected political speech. We cannot let our emotions jeopardize the free speech rights of Mr. Frazier or others who want to speak out against the war" (as quoted by the ACLU press release).

Back in 1985, the Supreme Court had decided in
*Cornelius v. NAACP Legal Defense and Educational
Fund* that there are three types of places in which the
exercise of speech and expression are to be closely
and carefully examined. They are the traditional public forum (such as a public street), a public forum
designated by the government, and the nonpublic
forum. Public streets have traditionally been considered a public forum for free speech and expression.
Frisby argued that the streets of Brookfield should be
considered a nonpublic forum. He said streets that
were residential and as physically narrow as
Brookfield's have never been designated as suitable or
proper venues for public communication and
demonstration.

The Court rejected this idea, saying that, "A public
street does not lose its status as a traditional public
forum simply because it runs through a residential
neighborhood." Yet the Court also concluded that
Brookfield's ordinance was "content neutral," meaning that it does not discriminate against certain points
of view, as Baton Rouge's parade policy did, in the
case of Reverend Cox. In addition, the Court said a
person's right not to be subjected to unwanted speech
should be protected. The Brookfield ordinance does
not ban picketing in residential neighborhoods. What
it does ban is the targeting of a particular resident, "in

David Bossie, president of the conservative activist group Citizens United, sits before a screen showing the group's film *Hillary: The Movie.*

an especially offensive way," and forcing that resident to hear unwanted speech.

In the end, the Supreme Court found that the value of being able to sit in one's home without being subjected to someone else's speech was sufficient to find the Brookfield ordinance acceptable under the Constitution.

When Corporations Engage in Political Speech

Does the first amendment only protect the speech of individuals? Or should groups like unions, nonprofits, and corporations also be able to speak freely?

During the 2008 presidential primary race, a conservative activist group called Citizens United decided to publicly oppose presidential candidate Hillary Clinton by airing a documentary critical of her. Citizens United planned to broadcast *Hillary: The Movie* on-demand and to advertise it on television. However, the U.S. District Court for the District of Columbia ruled that Citizens United's TV ads violated a provision of the McCain-Feingold Bipartisan Campaign Reform Act of 2002. This act made it illegal for corporations—including nonprofits and unions—to fund "electioneering communications" (broadcast ads that mention a candidate) thirty days before a primary and sixty days before a general election.

Citizens United complained that the law was too broad and could be abused. It appealed the district court's decision and took the case all the way to the Supreme Court. In a dramatic 5–4 decision, the Supreme Court found that it was unconstitutional for the government to prohibit corporations from funding political broadcasts. In other words, corporations have a right to free speech, just like people.

In his majority opinion, Justice Anthony Kennedy pointed out that because media companies are corporations, the McCain-Feingold Act could not be used to censor political speech in books, newspapers, and television shows. He saw no distinction between personal political speech and corporate political speech.

The dissenting justices worried that striking down McCain-Feingold would allow corporations to wield immense new power over the American electoral process. In a *New York Times* op-ed, David Kirkpatrick wrote: "A lobbyist can now tell any elected official: if you vote wrong, my company, labor union, or interest group will spend unlimited sums explicitly advertising against your re-election." The long-term effects of the Citizens United decision on the political process and outside organizations' control over campaigns and elections still remain to be seen.

DEFINING OBSCENITY

I t's easy to agree that the Constitution protects the right to express controversial ideas
or political opinions. But should it also protect speech that is offensive because it is
obscene? In the 1957 case *Roth v. United States*,
the Supreme Court ruled that "obscenity is not
within the area of constitutionally protected
speech or press." The case upheld the constitu-
tionality of a law that made it illegal to mail
material that was "obscene, lewd, lascivious, or
filthy...or other publication of an indecent char-
acter." But who decides what is obscene, lewd,
lascivious, or filthy?

More often than not, obscenity is subjective.
That is, not everyone agrees about what is
obscene. Something that one person finds offensive, another may find artistic. In the *Roth* case,
the Court also concluded that something could
be called obscene if the average person would
think that it really only appeals to people with
an unusual amount of sexual interest, depicts
sex in an offensive way, and lacks artistic, political, scientific, or literary value. Yet who is the
average person?

The government has decided that it is OK to restrict obscene speech in certain ways. Private companies, such as television stations, have the right to refuse to televise shows that the station owner finds offensive or otherwise problematic. In 1997, in *Reno v. ACLU*, the Supreme Court ruled that television broadcasters and cable operators can block certain programs that they deem potentially offensive to their audiences.

Yet these issues are never truly settled. Every decision whether or not to broadcast, display, or distribute potentially provocative material inevitably prompts outrage from one side or the other, charges of either censorship or obscenity, and hard questions with no easy answers about who gets to decide what is offensive or obscene and what is not, what "community standards" are, and exactly whose sensibilities within the community count more than those of others.

"ONE MAN'S VULGARITY IS ANOTHER MAN'S LYRIC"

On April 26, 1968, Paul Cohen was arrested for breaking California's Vulgar Speech Law. Cohen was in a public place, the Los Angeles County courthouse, wearing a jacket that used an obscene word to express his thoughts on the military draft and America's involvement in the Vietnam War.

Free speech counterprotesters in Denver, Colorado, oppose the message of another protest group, the Citizens for Peace and Respect, who were rallying against a Marilyn Manson concert. Controversy surrounds Manson, whose lyrics and stage presence are considered profane by some.

In the Los Angeles County Municipal Court, Cohen was found guilty and sentenced to thirty days in jail. When Cohen appealed the court's ruling, the California Court of Appeals upheld the verdict. The California Supreme Court declined to hear the case.

Cohen then requested a hearing with the U.S. Supreme Court, claiming that California had violated his rights by punishing him for displaying an antiwar message. He argued that his obscenely worded protest was protected by the First Amendment.

The Supreme Court found that the state could not punish Cohen for the underlying content or meaning of his message, as long as there was no obvious intent to disrupt the operation of the Selective Service or to encourage others to disobey the law. The Court held that the case was not about where he had worn the jacket (in the Los Angeles County courthouse), nor was it about obscenity, as there was nothing sexual about the words on the jacket. It was also not a case of "fighting words," as the message was not "directed to the person or the hearer," that is, not to anyone in particular with whom Cohen might start a fight.

The state of California maintained that it acted as it did to protect the sensibilities of its more sensitive citizens from the crudeness of Cohen's expression. Yet the Supreme Court countered that these citizens could simply ignore Cohen and his jacket and look away. They weren't being forced to "listen" to Cohen's "speech." The justices realized that if Cohen's speech were protected, the fact that some of his listeners in a public building might be unwillingly exposed to it does not justify Cohen's conviction for breach of peace. One justice even claimed that "one man's vulgarity is another man's lyric," and sometimes distasteful words are required to explicate inexpressible or overwhelmingly powerful emotions. Another justice reminded the state of California that the First Amendment does not only protect reasoned, responsible, and thoughtful speech, but also foolish, hotheaded, and ill-considered expression. He concluded by saying that if certain words are forbidden from public discourse, certain ideas will also be suppressed as a result.

As Cohen's case illustrates, speech takes many forms, both verbal and nonverbal. In fact, symbolic speech has long been contested in the courts.

"Offensively Lewd and Indecent Speech"

Nearly two decades after the Cohen case, the Supreme Court confronted the intersection of political speech and obscenity but arrived at a very different conclusion. On April 26, 1983, Matthew Fraser, a student at Bethel High School in Bethel, Washington, gave a speech in which he nominated a fellow student for an office in student government. His speech contained a number of sexual metaphors, describing how forceful and committed the candidate for office was.

Students reacted in a variety of ways during Fraser's speech. Some hooted and yelled. Some mimicked the sexual activities alluded to in the speech, and others appeared to be bewildered and embarrassed by his words. The assembly at which Fraser gave this speech was attended by about six hundred students,

Colorado State University student Joe Howard speaks out in support of an editorial that ran in the student newspaper that used an obscenity while discussing President George W. Bush. The paper's student editor was threatened with firing but ultimately received only a reprimand.

age fourteen to eighteen, all of whom were required to be there, unless they chose study hall instead.

Before the assembly, Fraser had discussed his speech with three teachers, two of whom told him that he probably should not deliver it, based upon its racy and inappropriate content. The teachers also informed Fraser that the speech could have serious consequences. Bethel High School does have a disciplinary rule forbidding the use of obscene and profane language and gestures. Significantly, none of the teachers Fraser spoke with told him that his speech might violate this school rule.

The next morning, Fraser was called to the assistant principal's office. The assistant principal informed him that his speech had violated the school rule against obscene language. Fraser admitted to having deliberately used sexual innuendo in his speech. The assistant principal suspended Fraser for three days and told him he would not be eligible to speak at graduation ceremonies at the end of the year.

Fraser went to the school's hearing officer to review the school's action. The hearing officer said that Fraser's speech was indecent and offensive in the eyes of many of the students and faculty in attendance at the assembly. Fraser served two days of his suspension and was allowed to return to school on the third day.

Meanwhile, E. L. Fraser, Matthew's father, took issue with the school's actions and brought the case to the federal district court, arguing that the school had violated his son's First Amendment right to free speech. Fraser's father further argued that because the school's disciplinary code said nothing about suspension as a punishment, the school had also violated his son's Fourteenth Amendment right to due process. The district court agreed with the Frasers, who won damages as well as Matthew Fraser's right to speak at commencement, which he did, on June 8, 1983.

The school district appealed the district court's decision. The court of appeals upheld the judgment of the district court, disagreeing with the school district's argument that Fraser's speech had a disruptive effect on the educational process. The school district also argued that it was trying to protect an audience of minors, who had no choice but to listen to the assembly speakers, from indecent, sexually explicit language in a setting sponsored by the school. Finally, in 1986 the Supreme Court ruled that Matthew Fraser's free speech rights had not been violated by the school's punishment of him. While acknowledging that school-age students retain their free speech rights on school property and are allowed to express unpopular or controversial views, they do not have the same latitude to express these views as adults do. Students must remain within the boundaries of socially acceptable behavior created and taught by their school and consider the sensitivities and sensibilities of their fellow students and other audience members.

ART OR OBSCENITY?

In September 1999, an art exhibit called "Sensation: Young British Artists from the Saatchi Collection," at the Brooklyn Museum in New York, featured explicit works such as a pig cut in half and suspended in a tank of formaldehyde and a bust of a man made from

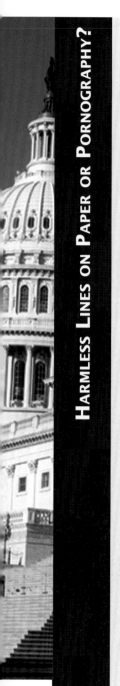

HARMLESS LINES ON PAPER OR PORNOGRAPHY?

Though comic books were once considered by many older Americans to be depraved and dangerous to the morals of young readers in the 1930s–1950s, today we are less accustomed to viewing graphic literature as a corrupting and dangerous influence. Yet in 2009, an avid American collector of Japanese manga named Christopher Handley was charged with mailing obscene matter (by buying and importing certain manga from Japan) and possessing obscene visual representations of sexual acts involving minors. By buying, receiving, and possessing this manga, Handley was in violation of a 2003 law called the Protect Act, which outlaws cartoons, drawings, sculptures, or paintings that depict sexual acts involving minors and have no "serious literary, artistic, political, or scientific value."

Handley was not in possession of any other materials that can be deemed pornographic, including photographs or movies. He only possessed manga, and the vast majority of his huge collection—tens of thousands of titles—was made up of more typical manga fare. He collected "everything that was out there that he could get his hands on," according to his lawyer. Yet Handley plead guilty to the charges and faced a maximum penalty of fifteen years in prison.

Other comic readers and collectors were stunned by Handley's arrest and conviction, seeing it as a major and unprecedented violation of free speech rights, an ill-informed designation of the material as obscene or pornographic, and a dangerous precedent for determining obscenity by gauging what the defendant's community would consider obscene. Charles Brownstein, executive director of the Comic Book Legal Defense Fund, argues that banning comic books will do nothing to prevent the abuse and exploitation that real pornography—particularly that found in photographic magazines and films—engenders. "The drawings are not obscene and are not tantamount to pornography. They are lines on paper" (as quoted by David Kravets in *Wired* magazine).

In 2010, Handley was sentenced to six months in prison, to be followed by three years of supervised release, five years of probation, and a psychological treatment program.

Even comic books, manga, and graphic novels are receiving increased scrutiny by authorities concerned with the widespread publication of indecent, obscene, or pornographic images or text, especially when viewed by minors.

nine pints of his own frozen blood. It also featured a portrait of a Roman Catholic icon, the Virgin Mary, adorned with clumps of dried elephant dung. The museum said it would not allow children under the age of seventeen to view the exhibit unless accompanied by an adult.

The mayor of New York, Rudolph Giuliani, threatened to close the museum. As a Roman Catholic, he professed to be deeply offended by the painting of the Virgin Mary. He described the art exhibit as "sick stuff." He also claimed it wasn't true art because he could easily make something similar, and he was no artist.

The issue became more complicated as Giuliani demanded that the museum shut down the exhibit. When the museum refused, the mayor turned his attention to the museum's age-restriction policy for "Sensation." Placing an age limit on admission to the show would violate the terms of the museum's lease, in a building owned by the city of New York. The lease states that museums housed in buildings owned by the city "shall at all reasonable times be free, open, and accessible to the public and private schools" of the city and "accessible to the general public on such terms of admission as the Mayor" sees fit. Giuliani pointed out that he was the mayor, and he didn't believe a taxpayer-funded public museum could restrict access to a certain group of people (children under the age of seventeen). While affirming artists' right to express anything they want to express, Giuliani claimed they didn't have the right to have their expressions—especially offensive ones—funded by taxpayers. He then threatened to withdraw the city's annual $7 million grant to the Brooklyn Museum and filed a lawsuit to evict the museum from its building.

In response, the museum's director filed a countersuit in federal court claiming that Mayor Giuliani was violating the Brooklyn Museum's First Amendment rights. Even

Chris Ofili's painting *The Holy Virgin Mary* was at the center of a controversy over obscenity that pitted New York City Mayor Rudy Giuliani against the Brooklyn Museum.

the U.S. Congress got involved, with the House of Representatives passing a resolution to halt federal funding of the museum. Museum curators nationwide, liberal newspaper editorial boards, the New York Civil Liberties Union, and many artists, actors, and writers expressed outrage at Giuliani's actions and suggested they were driven more by political grand-standing than genuine moral outrage but would nevertheless have a chilling effect upon the free exchange of ideas within the culture and society.

Finally, in November, U.S. district court judge Nina Gershon ruled that Mayor Giuliani had violated the First Amendment when he cut off city funds to the museum and began eviction proceedings against it. Gershon ordered the mayor and New York City to restore funding to the museum and to stop all attempts to evict the museum from its building or to interfere with the museum's board in any way. In her decision, she wrote that the city's court case was conceived and initiated to pressure the museum and that it is part of an ongoing effort to deny the museum's First Amendment rights simply because it was presenting ideas and images at odds with the government's vision of what was normal and acceptable.

SPEAKING IN SYMBOLS

There are many kinds of symbolic speech. Paul Cohen's jacket conveyed a very direct verbal message. But sometimes actions "speak" even louder than words. The marches, demonstrations, and sit-ins of the civil rights and Vietnam eras were all important forms not only of protest but also of symbolic, or nonverbal, speech. This chapter focuses on a number of important Supreme Court cases (and one from the court of appeals) that explicitly address the concept of symbolic speech, from saluting an outlawed flag (or refusing to salute the American flag) to wearing an unconventional hairstyle.

SYMBOL OF OPPOSITION

In 1928, nineteen-year-old Yetta Stromberg was charged and convicted of breaking a California law that forbade the displaying of red flags, banners, or badges that signify allegiance to a communist, socialist, or anarchist ideology and the promotion of government overthrow.

Stromberg was a member of the Young Communist League, an international organization

Students from Lincoln High in Vincennes, Indiana, salute the American flag. Flag saluting became mandatory at this school in the wake of the terrorist attacks of September 11, 2001.

that had ties to the Communist Party. She was also one of the supervisors of a summer camp for children between the ages of ten and fifteen in the San Bernardino Mountains, where she taught history and economics to the campers. More specifically, she taught her students to become more class-conscious, to favor the solidarity of workers. Stromberg maintained that workers were united by blood and were brothers and sisters in class struggle.

The charges brought against Stromberg centered on one of the camp's daily activities. Stromberg taught and led the children in a flag-raising ceremony. They raised a red flag, one made at the camp that was a reproduction of the flag of the Communist Party in the United States. The children stood, saluted the flag, and recited a pledge of allegiance to the red flag and "to the cause for which it stands, one aim throughout our lives, freedom for the working class."

The camp library also contained many books and pamphlets that espoused radical Communist dogma. California state officials argued that these books and pamphlets contained incitements to violence, armed uprisings, and class warfare. Stromberg did own some of these books, but she said they were not used for teaching at the camp, nor could it be proved that they were used to that end. She also claimed that she did not use the words "fostering sedition" or "anarchy" in her teaching of the children.

Stromberg was nevertheless convicted by the Superior Court of San Bernardino County. She appealed the decision in the California District Court of Appeals, and then petitioned for a hearing by the Supreme Court of California but was denied. She then brought her appeal before the U.S. Supreme Court. During her district court of appeals case, Stromberg argued that the California statute under which she had been convicted was unconstitutional. She insisted that the California statute against display of red flags was an unwarranted limitation on the right of free speech. Stromberg also argued that the California statute was a violation of the Fourteenth Amendment, which is designed to protect citizens from state laws that are unconstitutional.

The Supreme Court examined the California statute. The justices found in favor of Stromberg, concluding that she had not incited violence or government overthrow and that symbols of opposition to the government or prevailing political philosophy—like the red Communist flag—were a form of protected free speech. The government may not make opposition to itself illegal. In fact, the point of the free speech clause of the First Amendment is to protect Americans' right to oppose their government.

"TWO EARNEST CHRISTIAN CHILDREN"

On November 5, 1935, a young student named Billy Gobitas wrote a letter to school officials in Minersville, Pennsylvania, explaining his reason for refusing to salute the American flag in his classroom. As a "true follower of Christ," Billy believed that only God deserved his pledge of allegiance. Saluting the flag was akin to bowing down to another god, a form of idolatry that is forbidden by the Bible. He was careful to point out that he loved his country, but he loved God more and was bound to obey his commandments.

Billy's family belonged to the Jehovah's Witnesses, a religious sect not particularly popular in Minersville, where nearly 90 percent of the population was Roman Catholic. The Gobitas family did not become Witnesses until 1931, and at school, the Gobitas children saluted the flag until 1935.

Refusing to salute the flag was no small matter during this era. After World War I, American veterans formed an organization called the American Legion. As noted in Peter Irons's book *The Courage of Their Convictions: Sixteen Americans Who Fought Their Way to the Supreme Court*, the Legion began a campaign for "100 percent Americanism." This was a thinly veiled reactionary campaign against ethnic and racial minorities. They were joined eventually by the Veterans of Foreign Wars (VFW), the Daughters of the American Revolution (DAR), and the Ku Klux Klan (KKK). At the time, the Klan was trying to upgrade its image by aligning itself with so-called patriotic causes. By 1935, eighteen states had adopted flag-salute statutes. Hundreds of school boards across the country jumped on the patriotic bandwagon, voting to add the flag ceremony as a mandatory part of their curriculum.

According to Peter Irons, "In 1935, Jehovah's Witnesses became the first religious group to promote

Minersville, Pa.
Nov. 5, 1935

Our School Directors

Dear Sirs

    I do not salute the flag because I have promised to do the will of God. That means that I must not worship anything out of harmony with God's law. In the twentieth chapter of Exodus it is stated, "Thou shalt not make unto thee any graven image, nor bow down to them nor serve them for I the Lord thy God am a jealous God visiting the iniquity of the fathers upon the children

Billy Gobitas's 1935 letter to the Board of the Minersville School District explains his religious reasons for refusing to salute the American flag.

a campaign of refusal to join classroom ceremonies, and to press their challenges in court on a constitutional basis." The Witnesses' refusal to salute the flag in Nazi Germany (and general refusal to worship the state) landed more than ten thousand Witnesses in concentration camps during World War II (1939–1945).

Reacting to the experience of the German Jehovah's Witnesses, the leader of the American Witnesses, Joseph Rutherford, spoke against flag-saluting laws at the sect's national convention. Jehovah's Witnesses, he said, "do not 'Heil Hitler' or any other creature." Just a few days after Rutherford's speech, the Gobitas children, Lillian and Billy, decided they would not salute the flag. They could not be punished for this defiance, as neither the school nor the state had yet made the salute a requirement.

At the urging of school superintendent Charles Roudabush, however, the school board met, and it unanimously adopted a resolution that made the daily flag salute mandatory. Any refusal on the part of a student to take part in this ritual would be regarded as an act of insubordination and would be punished. Roudabush wasted no time in expelling the Gobitas children from the Minersville schools.

More than a year later, Walter Gobitas, Billy's father, took the school board to federal district court. He was represented by the ACLU and Jehovah's

Witness lawyers from the sect's New York headquarters. His complaint raised the issue of due process under the Fourteenth Amendment. Section One of the Fourteenth Amendment forbids the states from abridging or denying the privileges and immunities of U.S. citizens, depriving any person of life, liberty, or property without due process of law, and denying any person the equal protection of the law. Dozens of Supreme Court cases, dating from the 1890s, on matters of speech, religion, and assembly demonstrate that state and local governments are not allowed to limit any First Amendment rights that Congress would guarantee. The federal district court would be obliged to follow precedents set out by the Supreme Court in this area.

The school board's argument was that saluting the flag was not a religious ceremony but simply part of the curriculum meant to inculcate patriotism in the students. The board claimed it was protecting the health, safety, welfare, and morals of school students. The judge assigned to the case, Albert Maris, noted that the Pennsylvania state constitution's protection of rights of conscience was at issue. In drafting its constitution in 1776, Pennsylvania wanted to broaden the scope of the First Amendment, so the notion of rights of conscience had been included to expand protection of individual liberties to Pennsylvania citizens beyond what was provided for in the U.S. Constitution. The 1776 state constitution holds that "all men have a natural and unalienable right to worship Almighty God according to the dictates of their own consciences and understanding...And that no authority can or ought to be vested in, or assumed by any power whatever, that shall in any case interfere with, or in any manner control, the right of conscience in the free exercise of religious worship."

Consequently, in Maris's final opinion, he defended the rights of the individual over those of the group. He stated that it was "clear from the evidence that the refusal of these two earnest Christian children to salute the flag cannot even remotely prejudice or imperil the safety, health, morals, property or personal rights of their fellows" (as quoted by Irons). He ordered that the Gobitas children should be readmitted to the school with no requirement to participate in the flag salute.

The school board appealed this decision. The U.S. Court of Appeals upheld Maris's verdict. The judge in that case said, "Eighteen big states have seen fit to exert their power over a small number of little children...[The mandatory flag ceremony] happens to be abhorrent to the particular love of God of the little girl and boy now seeking our protection" (as quoted by Irons).

JEHOVAH'S WITNESSES AND FREEDOM OF SPEECH

The Jehovah's Witnesses organization has, in its history, argued in court a great deal for free speech rights. Consequently, it has managed to solidify protection of all Americans' First Amendment rights. According to religion and law scholar Eric Michael Mazur, in his book *The Americanization of Religious Minorities: Confronting the Constitutional Order*, "From 1938 to 1960, more than fifty cases involving members of the [Jehovah's Witnesses] organization reached the Supreme Court, producing more than thirty separate decisions on issues from flag-saluting to colportage [the selling or distributing of religious books]." The Jehovah's Witnesses believe that the only authority to which its members answer is God, and all earthly governments would eventually be overthrown by God. Such a belief system sets the stage for conflict with the local, state, and federal governments.

An early encounter with constitutional law took place in 1918, when the organization's then-president, Joseph Rutherford, was arrested for violating the Espionage Act of 1917. He was found guilty in federal district court of publishing (and distributing) materials that encouraged readers to resist the draft. However, the verdict was reversed by the federal court of appeals.

Other court cases involving the Jehovah's Witnesses' struggle to exercise their right to free speech and freedom of the press include:

- *Lovell v. City of Griffin* (1938) — protection of the right to distribute literature
- *Minersville v. Gobitas* (1940) — lost the right to refuse to salute the American flags in schools

- *Jones v. Opelika* (1943) — limits speech that might cause "a breach of the peace"
- *Jamison v. Texas* (1943) — the right to distribute printed material
- *Murdock v. Pennsylvania* (1943) — protection of colportage
- *West Virginia Board of Education v. Barnette* (1943) — right of free speech includes the right not to be forced to say what one does not believe, such as the Pledge of Allegiance
- *Wooley v. Maynard* (1977) — right not to support an ideology

The school board appealed again, and the case went before the U.S. Supreme Court in 1940. Members of the ACLU and the leader of the American Witnesses, Joseph Rutherford, testified on behalf of the Gobitas children. The Supreme Court found in favor of the Minersville school board. Possibly influenced by the oncoming threat of global war, the Court was moved to a show of patriotism by a vote of 8–1. Justice Felix Frankfurter wrote the Court's opinion that although "every possible leeway should be given to the claims of religious faith...[religion] does not relieve the citizen from the discharge of political responsibilities." Saluting the American flag could be seen as one of these unavoidable and obligatory political responsibilities. Frankfurter felt that the Supreme Court should not "exercise [its] judicial power unduly" by holding "too tight a rein" on state and local authorities.

Dissenting Justice Harlan Fiske Stone argued that laws that limit or put restrictions on personal liberties are generally aimed at politically helpless minorities. He held that the Constitution should certainly win out over "popular government," that is, state and local governments. This issue continues to divide the Court to this day.

At the end of this battle, however, the fight had only just begun. Within two weeks of the Court's decision, Jehovah's Witnesses were attacked all over the country. These attacks, some of them extremely violent, continued for two years after the Gobitas case, decreasing in number only when America's attention turned toward World War II.

"The Right to Differ"

The flag-saluting issue was revisited only three years later. In 1943, the Supreme Court agreed to hear the case of three children who lived near Charleston, West Virginia. Walter Barnette, Lucy McClure, and Paul Stull had been expelled from school for violating the state board of education's flag-salute policy. The Supreme Court's opinion took careful aim at Justice

Frankfurter's refusal to protect a person's First Amendment rights from the actions of local officials and electoral majorities. Frankfurter had said that civil and political obligations outweighed personal religious convictions. Justice Robert Jackson delivered the Court's decision, arguing that it is generally understood that censorship or suppression of expression of opinion is tolerated by the Constitution only when that expression poses "a clear and present danger of action of a kind the State is empowered to prevent and punish." Schoolchildren's passive silence during the salute of the flag does not constitute any such danger. In addition, just as the First Amendment protects an individual's right to express personal beliefs and opinions, it also protects the individual's right not to be forced—especially by the government or public authorities—to express beliefs he or she doesn't truly hold.

Justice Jackson further argued that public education must be religiously and politically neutral and not be supportive of or opposed to any class, creed, party, or faction. He concluded by insisting that an individual's belief system is not to be determined by a popular vote. In other words, even if the majority believes that all Americans should salute the flag, it is not allowed to use its size and power to force the minority to participate if it is unwilling to do so.

DRAWING THE LINE ON SPEECH ACTS

On March 31, 1966, there was a large Vietnam War protest outside a courthouse in South Boston, Massachusetts. One of the protesters, David O'Brien, publicly set fire to his draft card. A draft card is a certificate that verifies a person's registration with the Selective Service. The Federal Bureau of Investigation (FBI) arrested O'Brien and brought him to trial under a 1965 amendment to the Selective Service Act. The Universal Military Training and Service Act, a federal law, required all men between the ages of eighteen and twenty-six to register for service in the military.

Conscription, or required military registration, became a major social issue during the Vietnam War era. There were many demonstrations at draft boards and induction centers. Many people evaded the draft; thousands fled the country or went to prison. The amendment to this act that O'Brien was accused of violating called for as much as ten years in prison and a $10,000 fine for knowingly altering, forging, or mutilating a draft card.

O'Brien did not deny that he had burned his draft card. In fact, he told the FBI agents that he had done so to express his beliefs. He knowingly broke a federal law to engage in symbolic speech. In the U.S. District Court, O'Brien said the 1965 amendment was a

Antiwar protesters burn their draft cards in a 1972 protest against the Vietnam War and the draft on the steps of the Pentagon in Arlington, Virginia.

violation of his First Amendment right to free speech. He had burned the card, he said, in order to persuade other people to reevaluate the Selective Service Act and arrive at the conclusion that draft resistance was necessary.

Nevertheless, the federal district court decided that the Selective Service Act Amendment was indeed constitutional—and they found O'Brien guilty. He appealed the decision to the U.S. Court of Appeals, which overturned his conviction and declared the 1965 amendment to be unconstitutional. The

Department of Justice then appealed the Court of Appeals' decision to overturn O'Brien's conviction to the U.S. Supreme Court. The justices ruled against O'Brien, arguing that the 1965 amendment to the Selective Service Act does not infringe upon free speech; it merely forbids the knowing destruction of certificates (draft cards) issued by the Selective Service System. The Supreme Court did not find draft card burning to be an act of symbolic speech; it was merely an act of destruction.

Just twenty-five years after the Barnette case, the Supreme Court, under Chief Justice Earl Warren, reinterpreted the notion of symbolism. The justices viewed the act of burning the draft card as just that—an act, not a form of speech. The amendment to the Selective Service Act prohibits knowingly destroying the card but says nothing about speech. Warren approached the issue with a very literal and conservative interpretation of what constitutes "speech." Justice Warren remarked that a law prohibiting destruction of Selective Service draft cards no more violates the right to free speech than does a motor vehicle law prohibiting the destruction of drivers' licenses.

O'Brien had argued that the amendment was unconstitutional because of the way it was used to convict him—it was used, he said, to suppress freedom of speech. O'Brien maintained that what he did was protected as symbolic speech and that the First

Amendment guarantees the communication of ideas through one's conduct or actions. In this case, O'Brien's conduct—his burning of the draft card—served as a demonstration of his opposition to the war in Vietnam and the draft being used to supply it with young soldiers. The Supreme Court explicitly rejected the notion that almost any kind of conduct or action can be labeled "speech" that conveys the perpetrator's ideas. Furthermore, when speech and nonspeech elements are combined in the course of a single action, the government may have a compelling enough interest in regulating the nonspeech elements—the individual's conduct, especially if criminal—to justify placing limits on First Amendment freedoms. The Warren court insisted on drawing the line somewhere between speech and nonspeech "events." Otherwise, no actions could ever be considered unlawful. Every action, no matter how outrageous, violent, dangerous, antisocial, or anarchic, could be considered a protected form of speech and the free expression of a personal or political idea.

Flag Desecration as Religious Protest

The state of Nebraska has had a law banning the burning of the American flag on its book since the 1970s. Under this law, it is a misdemeanor to treat the

Members of Fred Phelps Westboro Baptist Church protest the funeral of Army Private First Class Cory Hiltz by picketing and trampling on American flags. Church members believe military deaths reflect God's wrath against a sinful America.

flag with "contempt or ridicule" by "mutilating, defacing, defiling, burning, or trampling" on it. The law survived even after the Supreme Court's 1988 decision that flag burning was a protected form of symbolic speech. The state law may have finally met its match, however, in 2010, when it was challenged by members of the Westboro Baptist Church of Topeka, Kansas, led by Pastor Fred Phelps.

Phelps and his church believe that God is punishing the United States for its toleration of sins such as homosexuality. They express these beliefs by burning American flags, as well as picketing the funeral of deceased soldiers (the large numbers of casualties from the wars in Iraq and Afghanistan are further proof, according to Phelps, of God's wrath for America).

In Westboro Baptist's lawsuit against Nebraska, it describes the state's flag law as "a content-based restriction on speech" designed only to "prohibit the expression of specific viewpoints" (as quoted by Bob Allen of the American Baptist Press). A federal judge from the U.S. District Court agreed and barred Nebraska from enforcing the flag desecration law against the Westboro Baptist protesters, as long as these church members "otherwise act peacefully while desecrating the American or Nebraska flag during their religiously motivated protests" (as quoted by the American Baptist Press).

PROTECTING HATE SPEECH

Unfortunately, there are many prejudiced people in America who discriminate against women, racial, ethnic, and religious minorities, immigrants, and gays and lesbians. The expression of their antipathy for certain groups of people is often described as hate speech. Some First Amendment scholars argue that hate speech ought to be censored because it hurts the targeted person or group of people on an emotional and psychological level and may incite physical violence. Moreover, hate speech diminishes the community or social standing of the targeted group, often promulgating negative stereotypes, making them further vulnerable to physical and verbal attacks.

This strategy of making hate speech illegal raises many vexing constitutional issues, however. After all, placing limits on speech is difficult. Who decides precisely what the speech means and how it is received? How would limits be enforced? What kinds of words are threatening, intimidating, or harassing, and, therefore, subject to legal action?

Some scholars argue that the reaction of targeted individuals to hate speech depends entirely on the individual. Some people will be frightened or intimidated; others will be inspired to take action. Some people will be silenced by hate speech, but there are others who respond by boldly voicing their views. Rather than force haters into silence, some argue that they should be educated instead. Their hateful speeches should be met with opposing, enlightened speeches. So, to paraphrase Supreme Court Justice Louis Brandeis, the answer to hateful speech is not enforced silence, but more speech.

FREE TO HATE

Hate speech was at the heart of a case concerning Clarence Brandenburg, the leader of a KKK group in Ohio. Brandenburg gave a speech at a KKK rally on the outskirts of Cincinnati. The event was filmed, and parts of the speech were shown on television. People who watched the broadcast saw twelve figures in white hoods, some holding shotguns. They were gathered around a burning cross, listening to Brandenburg. The leader's speech was full of hateful messages, including, "Send the Jews back to Israel!" and "Freedom for whites!"

Brandenburg was tried in an Ohio state court under a law that made it illegal to urge others to

Clarence Brandenburg *(left)*, an officer of the Ku Klux Klan (KKK), and Richard Hanna, a member of the American Nazi Party, pose together after their 1964 arrest in Cincinnati, Ohio. They were charged with disturbing the peace and inciting violence during a KKK rally.

commit acts of violence and terrorism as a method of bringing about political change. The law also made it illegal to gather with others to teach or support the use of violence and force. Brandenburg was convicted, but he appealed to Ohio's supreme court and subsequently to the U.S. Supreme Court. The Supreme Court justices looked carefully at what Brandenburg had said—that if the federal government continued to "suppress the white, Caucasian race" some "revengeance" would have to be taken. The justices also looked at the state law Brandenburg was accused of breaking.

The Supreme Court decided that a law that punishes advocacy—the encouraging of others to act in support of one's beliefs or agenda—is unconstitutional. So, too, is a law that does not allow assembly with others to advocate action. Such a law violates both the First and Fourteenth Amendments. As a result, the Supreme Court overturned Charles Brandenburg's conviction.

FIGHTING WORDS

On April 6, 1940, Walter Chaplinsky, a Jehovah's Witness, stood outside the city hall of Rochester, New Hampshire. There he passed out literature and announced to passersby that all religion is a racket. Angry citizens began to complain, so Rochester City Marshal James Bowering warned Chaplinsky not to start a riot, threatening him with arrest. In response to this threat, Chaplinsky allegedly said, "You are a [expletive] racketeer" and a "damned Fascist," and "the whole government of Rochester are Fascists."

Bowering arrested Chaplinsky for breaking New Hampshire's "fighting words" law. The law reads as follows: "No person shall address any offensive, derisive, or annoying word to any other person who is lawfully in any street or other public place, nor call him by any offensive or derisive name, nor make any noise or exclamation in his presence and hearing with intent to deride, offend, or annoy him, or to prevent him from pursuing his lawful business or occupation."

Chaplinsky was found guilty and appealed the verdict, which was upheld by the New Hampshire Supreme Court. Chaplinsky argued that the fighting words statute limited freedom of speech, freedom of the press, and freedom of worship. He also claimed that the law was vague and indefinite. The case, on appeal again, finally went to the U.S. Supreme Court in 1942.

The Court turned its attention to the New Hampshire law, carefully discussing the limits of free speech. It pointed out that historically the right to free speech has not been seen as absolute at all times and in every situation. Certain forms of speech have long been considered worthy of prevention and punishment. This class of unprotected speech has included the lewd and obscene, the profane, the libelous, and the insulting ("fighting words" that personally injure the individual they are directed at and tend to create an immediate disturbance of the peace).

The purpose of Ohio's fighting words law was to keep the peace, with no words forbidden except those that tend to precede or cause acts of violence against the person to whom the fighting words are addressed. The Ohio law does not define "offensive" words according to an individual's reaction to them, but by "what men of common intelligence would understand would be words likely to cause an average person to fight."

Because the Supreme Court supported the notion that it is possible to define a class of words that would be likely to start a fight or instigate violence, it held that the New Hampshire statute was legal and that it did not violate Chaplinsky's right to free speech. Obviously, distinguishing between speech, action, and speech that inspires action can become quite difficult.

SYMBOLS OF HATE

Symbols have often been found by the courts to qualify as protected speech if they are worn or displayed in a public place, before a general audience—even if they are symbols associated with hate speech like swastikas or burning crosses. However, the First Amendment does not protect such symbols when they are used to desecrate private property, such as burning a cross on someone else's lawn or spray painting a swastika on a synagogue.

In 1992, in *R. A. V. v. City of St. Paul, Minnesota*, the U.S. Supreme Court struck down a St. Paul, Minnesota, ordinance that prohibited cross burning. The city felt that because white supremacist groups historically have used cross burnings to intimidate the targets of their wrath—particularly African Americans—symbolic acts such as cross burnings should be banned. The Supreme Court stated that the city cannot prosecute someone for the content of his or her speech in such a case, but that it could arrest the cross-burner for criminal trespass and harassment.

SPEECH CODES ON CAMPUS

Several notable incidents involving hate speech have occurred on the

Members of the white supremacist group the National Socialist Movement hold an anti-immigration rally in Riverside, California. In the United States, symbols of hate, like the Nazi swastika, are protected forms of speech in certain contexts.

campuses of American colleges and universities. Starting in the 1980s, many schools anxious to respond to this problem adopted speech codes prohibiting speech that could offend any group of people, based on race, gender, sexual orientation, ethnicity, or religion. These speech codes were often written using very broad language, and many were later challenged and struck down by courts.

The ACLU opposes speech codes, arguing that hate speech must be protected to keep other forms of more palatable but still controversial political speech from being threatened. Critics of hate speech ordinances like the ACLU point out that colleges are, after all, not just places where students take classes, but intellectual centers dedicated to the exchange of ideas. Students must learn to sift good ideas from bad and evaluate the validity and worth of propositions. As part of this process, they will be confronted with offensive, hateful, and plain stupid ideas, but an important part of their education is being able to identify the weaknesses, faulty logic, and false and erroneous arguments underlying such ideas. Not all the ideas young people are exposed to at college are positive, nor will students agree with everything they hear. What if hate speech inhibits the educational experience of the students that it targets, such as women, racial and religious minorities, and lesbians and gays?

The ACLU has opposed any policies on college campuses that restrict speech. It has challenged university speech codes at the University of Connecticut, the University of Michigan, the University of Wisconsin, and the University of California. The ACLU believes that all members of the academic community have the right to hold and to express views that others may find hateful, offensive, or emotionally upsetting. The ACLU encourages colleges and universities to deal with bigotry through education and speech, not through censorship. It believes that freedom of thought and expression is particularly important on college campuses, which should be devoted to creating a spirit of shared inquiry, intellectual honesty, and tolerance for the ideas and opinions of others, even when these are opposed to one's own and are hateful or offensive.

Today, many universities and colleges have dropped speech codes in favor of antiharassment policies or codes of conduct. These new rules are written to specifically target hate speech, rather than speech that is simply distasteful or offensive. But many free speech advocates still find any policy that limits speech on campus troubling.

In its publication *Spotlight on Speech Codes 2010*, the Foundation for Individual Rights in Education (FIRE) surveyed 375 American universities and found

TERRY JONES AND "INTERNATIONAL BURN A KORAN DAY"

Freedom of speech means nothing if it only protects speech and ideas that nearly all Americans agree with anyway. In fact, Americans' true commitment to the First Amendment is tested by speech they find hateful, offensive, or even dangerous.

In 2010, Terry Jones, the pastor of the tiny Dove World Outreach Center church in Gainesville, Florida, declared September 11 to be "International Burn a Koran Day." He announced he was planning a Koran bonfire to express his conviction that "Islam is of the devil." His plan symbolically blamed the terrorist attacks of September 11, 2001, on Islam as a religion —not merely on the actions of a few radical terrorists.

Many Americans were offended by this condemnation of the world's second largest religion and disturbed by the idea of book burning, which harkens back to the methods of Nazi rallies and the

Pastor Terry Jones of the Dove World Outreach Center holds a news conference relating to his call for an "International Burn a Koran Day."

Spanish Inquisition. Jones's plan also sparked an international uproar, inspiring protests as far afield as Jakarta, Indonesia, and Kabul, Afghanistan. Yet Jones's constitutional right to hold his Koran bonfire was clearly protected under the First Amendment.

Finally, Defense Secretary Robert Gates called Jones to warn him that his demonstration could place American troops in Iraq and Afghanistan at risk. Jones also received a call from a Muslim community leader, who offered to discuss moving a controversial Islamic community center slated to open near Ground Zero, in Lower Manhattan, the former site of the World Trade Center that was destroyed by two hijacked planes on September 11. Following his conversation with Gates, Jones cancelled International Burn a Koran Day. However, the incident was a powerful reminder that freedom of speech is a right that must be used responsibly.

that 71 percent had earned a "red light," signifying that they have "at least one policy that both clearly and substantially restricts freedom of speech, or bars public access to [its] speech-related policies." However, FIRE also found that the number of schools imposing speech codes is on the decline.

HATEFUL LYRICS

Hate speech is not confined to the written word, spoken rants, or Internet postings. It can show up in popular music, too. Gay rights groups have protested

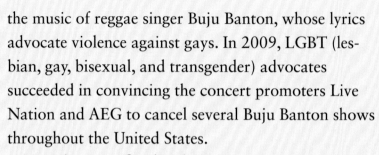

the music of reggae singer Buju Banton, whose lyrics advocate violence against gays. In 2009, LGBT (lesbian, gay, bisexual, and transgender) advocates succeeded in convincing the concert promoters Live Nation and AEG to cancel several Buju Banton shows throughout the United States.

But there is a fine line between promoting responsible business practices and censoring an artist. Banton has an undeniable right to sing about anything he wants to—but his promoters have the right to refuse to present messages they disagree with or find objectionable. The rap musician Eminem has come under fire repeatedly for making derogatory remarks about women and gays in his songs. Nevertheless, he is more popular than ever, and many argue that his art is absolutely protected by the First Amendment.

HATE SPEECH ONLINE

An increasing number of Web sites contain or are devoted to hate speech. Thanks to the anonymity of the Internet, hateful ideas, comments, jokes, rumors, and "memes" (essentially ideas that "go viral") can spread like wildfire. The people who participate in the conversation are almost never held accountable for their words, ideas, or opinions, or for the actions they may inspire in others.

In 2010, the Simon Wiesenthal Center, a research and educational organization, published *Digital*

Buju Banton performs on Randall's Island in New York City. Banton has attracted controversy and protest because of his homophobic lyrics.

Terrorism and Hate 2010, a DVD report on Internet hate speech and activity. The center discovered 11,500 Web sites, forums, and networks that spread hate and racism or promoted terrorist ideas and activities. Even more remarkable, the number of hateful sites had grown 20 percent since the previous year. Among the troubling Web content that the center uncovered were a video game in which players could bomb victims of the massive 2010 earthquake in Haiti, video tutorials on how to build homemade bombs, and Web forums riddled with hateful messages.

Is it imperative or even possible for these sites to be suppressed by law? There is no clear answer, especially because there is no ultimate gatekeeper of the

SPEECH NOT PROTECTED UNDER THE FIRST AMENDMENT

- Unwanted speech (words directed specifically at someone who does not want to hear them)
- Obscene speech
- Fighting words (words that will, or are intended to, start a fight)
- Personal threats
- Fraudulent speech
- Slander (spoken false statements that hurt others' reputations)
- Libel (printed false statements that hurt others' reputations)

Internet. Some advocate the censorship of hate messages on the Web, but others, such as members of the ACLU, argue for the protection of free speech rights of all Americans, no matter how hateful their speech. Norman Siegel, executive director of the New York Civil Liberties Union, argues that censorship of any kind is the enemy of free speech and a democratic society. Any speech that is free to be uttered on a street corner should also be permitted on the Internet, which is simply a virtual parallel world, a "marketplace of ideas," not a specialized venue that requires unique or extraordinary protections against offensive or hateful ideas, according to Siegel. The same principles and rules that govern public speech in the "real" world should apply to Internet discourse.

FREEDOM OF SPEECH
AND YOUR DAILY LIFE

The Supreme Court's rulings on First Amendment cases have a direct effect on the everyday lives of all Americans. Take, for instance, Mary Beth Tinker's black armband. She can be said to have paved the way for people to wear red ribbons for AIDS awareness, pink ribbons to support breast cancer research, and yellow ribbons to support people in the military (not to mention T-shirts emblazoned with images of revolutionaries like Che Guevara or slogans mocking the president of the United States). There are even ribbons that represent support of free speech rights; many Web sites show a blue ribbon to support free speech online.

HAIR HYSTERIA

Does your school have rules about how you dress? Does it have rules about your hairstyle, too? In 1972, a case went before the U.S. Court of Appeals for the Second Circuit about just that—acceptable hairstyles. Joseph Massie and a number of other male students were suspended from Tuscola High School in North Carolina. They had failed to obey a school

guideline that regulated hair length and length of sideburns. The president of the student body asked for the
passage of such a regulation in response to a specific
incident.

A fight had occurred when one student had called
another with long hair a hippie. Two other long-haired
students reported that they had been threatened by
other students. Teachers complained about the long-
haired students. One said Massie and the others had
trouble writing on the board in class because their
hair was in their eyes, and an industrial arts teacher
claimed he would not let the long-haired boys into his
shop class for safety reasons.

Massie and the others wore their hair past their
collars and covering their ears, and at least two of the
boys had sideburns that extended below their ears.
They objected to the school's attempt to regulate their
personal appearance and took their case against the
chairman of the board of education, Stanley Henry, to
federal district court. The court said no constitutional
rights had been violated and dismissed the case. On
appeal, it went to the federal court of appeals, where-
upon the decision was reversed. Circuit Judge Ralph
Winter delivered the verdict, reminding the public that
the founding fathers, Generals Grant and Lee, and
Jesus Christ all wore their hair long and/or had "ful-
some" sideburns. None of these august personages
would have been allowed to attend Tuscola Senior

Claudius Benson II was suspended from the Old Redford Academy in Detroit, Michigan, because of his hair, which he wore long for religious reasons. The ACLU took up his case, and he was eventually readmitted to the school.

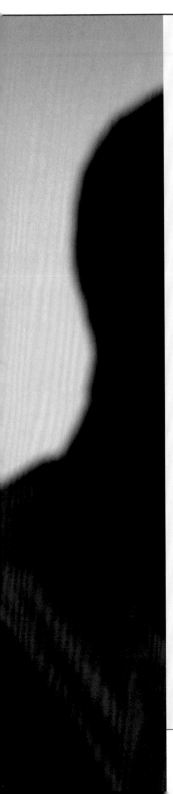

High School, calling into serious question the validity and worth of the school's regulation.

The judge also pointed out that there was some confusion about which part of the Constitution protects a person's right to wear his or her hair how he or she chooses. He also noted that such an issue is rather silly, as the way a person's hair looks is most often determined by the fashion of the time in which the person lives.

Judge Winter went on to enumerate cases focusing on similar issues. In *Ferrell v. Dallas Independent School District* (1968), the court upheld the validity of a school rule forbidding a "Beatle-type haircut," and in *Jackson v. Dorrier* (1970), the court held that there was no violation of the First Amendment when long hair was outlawed as a result of it having caused classroom disturbance. In other cases, he said, the right to have hair of whatever length a person chooses was shown to be a right of due process under both the First and Ninth Amendments. The Ninth Amendment protects individual rights not specifically spelled out elsewhere in the Constitution. Judge Winter went on to argue that a commitment to decency and good behavior did not require a short haircut for boys and men, that the perceived unattractiveness of long hair on males doesn't justify banning it, and forced conformity to conventional standards of appearance is not a part of the educational process that should be valued or encouraged. He concluded by taking a swipe at the school's teachers and administrators. Any disturbance created by the boys' long hair could have been quelled or prevented altogether if the school had promoted, emphasized, and enforced an attitude of tolerance among both faculty and students, rather than one of suppression and derision. On a practical note, he added that it would be within the school's rights to ask the long-haired students to tie back their hair for safety reasons. Otherwise, however, Massie and the other long-haired male students were vindicated and their complaint was won.

FREE TO INQUIRE

In 1976, the Island Trees School Board of Long Island, New York, banned a number of books from its junior and senior high school libraries. The titles were the anonymously written *Go Ask Alice*, Alice Childress's

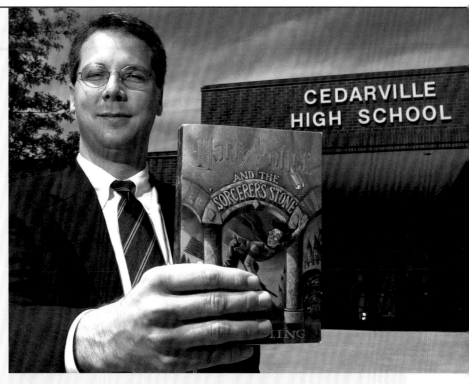

Attorney Brian Meadors stands outside Cedarville High School in Cedarville, Arkansas, with a copy of *Harry Potter and the Sorcerer's Stone*. The school board had banned the Harry Potter series from the school library. Meadors successfully represented parents who opposed this book banning and censorship.

A Hero Ain't Nothin' But a Sandwich, Eldridge Cleaver's *Soul on Ice*, an anthology edited by Langston Hughes called *The Best Short Stories of Negro Writers*, Desmond Morris's *The Naked Ape*, Piri Thomas's *Down These Mean Streets*, Kurt Vonnegut's *Slaughterhouse-Five*, and Richard Wright's *Black Boy*. The school board said that its duty was to "protect the children in [their] schools from this moral danger as surely as from physical and medical dangers." In fact, school board members said it was their "moral obligation" to prevent students from reading books they deemed to be anti-American, anti-Christian, anti-Semitic, vulgar, immoral, and "just plain filthy."

Steven Pico was an Island Trees student, and he (along with some other students) took the school board to court for violating his First Amendment right to read the speech of others. He demanded that the books be returned to the library. The U.S. District Court sided with the school board. When the case went to the court of appeals, Pico won. The board appealed, and the case went before the U.S. Supreme Court in 1982.

The Court addressed the essential issue of the case: does the First Amendment limit a school board's right to remove books from junior and senior high school libraries? Justice William Brennan, who delivered the opinion of the Court, first pointed out that the students were not looking to restrict the school board's power over in-class curricula. Rather, Pico and the other students simply objected to the school board banning library books, books that are optional, rather than required, reading. In addition, Pico and the other students were only challenging the board's right to remove books placed there by school authorities; they were not demanding that the board add new books to the library. The Court agreed that local school boards had the authority to develop and apply curriculum in a way that would enable the transmission of community values, but they must do so while respecting students' First Amendment rights.

Justice Brennan continued by arguing that public schools are supposed to offer free access (within reason) to information and ideas. Therefore, their mandate is not to restrict or narrow the range of available knowledge. Such a practice is fundamentally opposed to an educational mission. Brennan pointed out that traditionally and in most contexts, the Supreme Court has held that the Constitution protects the right to receive information and ideas. This is true even for school-age Americans.

Brennan went on to argue that an individual's right to receive ideas comes directly from another's right to communicate them; you can not have one without the other. He also described the unique role of a school library as a place where students can explore the unknown. It is a place where students can expand on curriculum material and go beyond it; it is the place where they "remain free to inquire." Justice Brennan concluded that school boards can determine the content of their school libraries. But their decisions about which books to place on the shelves and which to ban can't be based upon narrow political

BANNED IN THE USA

Freedom of speech does more than protect one's right to say what he or she wishes to say—it also protects access to the opinions and ideas of others. Many classics of modern literature, such as Mark Twain's *Adventures of Huckleberry Finn*, James Joyce's *Ulysses*, Ernest Hemingway's *For Whom the Bell Tolls*, F. Scott Fitzgerald's *The Great Gatsby*, John Steinbeck's *Grapes of Wrath* and *Of Mice and Men*, John Knowles's *A Separate Peace*, George Orwell's *1984* and *Animal Farm*, and William Golding's *The Lord of the Flies* were once banned and even burned by some school boards and townships because local censors considered them obscene, politically subversive, or otherwise dangerous and objectionable, and feared that they would offend and corrupt the public. Some of these books were even banned for sale, importation, and mailing within the entire United States. Thanks to the First Amendment, however, most of the bans on these books were eventually lifted (though some school boards continue to forbid these and other books).

Despite the First Amendment, censorship and book banning is still alive and well in the United States. Every year, hundreds of books are removed from school library shelves after parents challenge them, or complain that they find the books inappropriate. The American Library Association's annual Banned Books Week began in 1982, at a time when the challenging of the presence of certain books in school and public libraries by parents, school administrators, and other community members began to increase dramatically. Since then, more than one thousand titles have been challenged in every state in the country.

During 2010's Banned Books Week, the American Library Association released figures concerning book challenges for 2009. In 2009 alone, there were 460 attempts to remove materials from libraries. That year, three particular books appeared on the top of the most frequently challenged list, as they have done for years, despite being both popular and widely acclaimed classics of young adult literature. These were J. D. Salinger's *The Catcher in the Rye*, Harper Lee's *To Kill a Mockingbird*, and Alice Walker's *The Color Purple*. They were joined near the top of the list by relative newcomers—J. K. Rowling's Harry Potter series, Stephanie Meyer's Twilight series, and Khaled Hosseini's *The Kite Runner*.

beliefs or affiliations or out of a desire to purge a library of ideas the school board disagrees with or dislikes. The Constitution does not permit the official suppression of ideas, even among minors.

Steven Pico's case did not bring an end to efforts to restrict the free flow of ideas in this country. Today, many individuals and groups are still working to regulate young people's access to certain books, television and radio programs, movies, and works of art.

AN ONGOING BATTLE

Though the Gobitas family fought for the right for objecting schoolchildren to refuse to salute the

American flag, this right is not yet fully protected and thus the debate over it rages on. According to the Freedom Forum, an organization devoted to protecting the rights of all Americans, a movement to enforce the daily recital of the Pledge of Allegiance is currently gaining steam.

In 1998, a sixteen-year-old in Florida refused to stand and recite the pledge. He was angry at the way the government had treated his father, a Marine Corps veteran with cancer. He was suspended from school for a day. That same year, in Seattle, Washington, a thirteen-year-old Jehovah's Witness refused to say the Pledge for religious reasons, and his teacher sent him outside to stand in the rain for fifteen minutes.

In 2000, a high school student from Alabama raised his fist during the Pledge (a symbol of Black Power) and was paddled by a school administrator. He was supporting a fellow student who had made a similar protest just one day earlier.

Since the events of September 11, 2001, many state legislatures have proposed new laws to compel all students to recite the Pledge of Allegiance. In 2002, Colorado lawmakers announced that all students in public school would be absolutely required to participate in the Pledge of Allegiance. Only students whose religions forbade them to recite the pledge or students whose parents had given them permission could sit out the pledge.

The rights of these students were clearly violated; in 1943, the Supreme Court ruled that forcing children to recite the pledge against their personal beliefs is to deny them their freedom. Colorado's new law was challenged in federal court by the ACLU. After the trial, Colorado's legislature revised the law so that students could decide for themselves to refrain from reciting the Pledge of Allegiance without threat of punishment.

STUDENT SPEECH ONLINE

The Supreme Court has ruled that school officials have a right to regulate nonpolitical student speech that disrupts a learning environment. But can school officials discipline students who post offensive material online, after school hours, from home on personal, nonschool computers? Two recent cases tested this new social and scholastic problem.

In 2005, a Pennsylvania high school honor student created an insulting fake MySpace profile for her principal. Although this profile was created off-campus and after school hours, the student was suspended for ten days. A federal judge overturned the suspension, saying that the school couldn't punish student speech outside school, especially since the profile did not disrupt the school's learning environment.

However, in 2007, a Pennsylvania junior high school student also created a mock MySpace profile for her principal, describing the principal as a

Social networking sites, blogs, chat rooms, and other Internet forums are becoming the new, hotly contested front lines in the perpetual battle between advocates of free speech and defenders of decency and privacy.

pedophile. She, too, was suspended for ten days. When her parents sued, Third Circuit Court judges sided with the school, saying the profile was so outrageous that it distracted other students from their studies.

So what is important—where student speech takes place? Or how disruptive student speech is? Only time will tell what the courts will decide.

DECENCY AND FREE SPEECH ON THE INTERNET

In response to some highly publicized cases of children being exposed to pornographic material online, lawmakers began to argue for laws that would regulate content on the Internet. The Communications Decency Act (CDA) was enacted by Congress as part of the Telecommunications Decency Act of 1996. The CDA did three things:

- It made illegal the transmission of any comment, request, suggestion, proposal, image, or other communication that is obscene, lewd, lascivious, filthy, or indecent, with intent to annoy, abuse, threaten, or harass another person.
- It also made it illegal to transmit such material if the person transmitting it knows the receiver to be under eighteen.
- Any expression that shows or describes sexual or excretory activities or organs and is available to anyone under eighteen was also deemed illegal.

Yet, these guidelines turned out to be overly broad, rendering illegal many worthwhile texts and other communications. For example, any Web pages, newsgroups, chat rooms, and online discussion that referenced and/or quoted J. D. Salinger's *The Catcher in the Rye* could be considered in violation of the law, given that novel's occasional use of vulgar language and fleeting references to "sexual or excretory activities or organs."

In 1997, the Supreme Court struck down the CDA in *Reno, Attorney General of the United States et al. v. American Civil Liberties Union*. The Court ruled that the Internet is unique and entitled to the highest protection under the First Amendment. This gives information and ideas shared on the Internet the same protections that apply to printed material.

Congress did not give up on trying to protect children online, however. The 1998 Child Online Protection Act (COPA) was intended to limit children's access to harmful materials online. Harmful materials would be defined by "contemporary community standards" and could range from pornographic videos to legitimate works of art with sexual content, like nude paintings. COPA ordered Web site operators who distributed such materials to prevent minors from accessing their sites.

In 1999, COPA was struck down by the Third Circuit Court of Appeals, which ruled that the act's definition of harmful materials was so broad that it infringed on the First Amendment. However, the Supreme Court was not so sure it agreed. It asked the Third Circuit Court to review the case again. Following this review, COPA was again struck down.

Yet COPA was not dead yet. It was finally brought before the Supreme Court in 2004, in a case called *Ashcroft v. American Civil Liberties Union*. The Supreme Court ruled that the bill's stated purpose, protecting kids on the Internet, would be better achieved through other means, such as online filters (in fact, in 2003, the Supreme Court upheld the Children's Internet Protection Act, which requires public and school libraries that receive government Internet discounts to install filters on their computers to block pornography). The COPA case returned to the lower courts, where COPA was struck down twice more. In 2009, the Supreme Court declined to hear the case again, killing COPA once and for all. The courts had found that the same freedom of speech that governs ordinary life should apply to speech on the Internet.

PARENTAL DISCRETION ADVISED: THE V-CHIP

In response to the outcry that many television shows watched by children contain objectionable material, the federal government has been looking to technology for a method of blocking certain shows. Within the Federal Communication Commission's (FCC) Telecommunications Act of 1996, Congress included a provision called "Parental Choice in Television

Programming," commonly known as the V-chip law. The law requires television networks to give their shows ratings that indicate the level of sexual content, violence, explicit language, or otherwise problematic content within the show, similar to the way in which movies are rated.

Currently, homes can be equipped with a device that allows parents to block reception of programs that are rated as overly sexual, violent, or problematic. Yet this seemingly helpful tool for concerned parents is also a free speech concern, according to the Freedom Forum. In the V-chip law itself, there was no mention of which shows were to be rated and who was going to do the rating. Critics of the V-chip law assert that this legislation is a form of censorship and an intrusion by the federal government into television programming. In 1997, in response to the V-chip law, television industry executives proposed their own ratings system. Parents' organizations and others disliked these ratings because they felt that they were not sufficiently descriptive.

Proponents of the V-chip law maintain that it was merely intended to help parents control and be knowledgeable about what their children watch. Yet opponents of the law see it as encroaching upon the individual's basic rights. They argue that the government doesn't have the right to monitor and censor what appears on television. Caroline Fredrickson, of

- TV-Y7: designated for children age seven and over
- TV-G: suitable for entire audience; parents may leave children unattended
- TV-PG: parental guidance suggested as program may contain material that some parents may find unsuitable for younger children
- TV-14: parents strongly cautioned as program may contain infrequent coarse language, limited violence, and some suggestive sexual dialogue and situations
- TV-M: designed for mature audiences and may contain profane language, graphic violence, and explicit sexual content

the American Civil Liberties Union, believes that "the government should not replace parents as decision makers in America's living rooms. There are some things that the government does well. But deciding what is aired and when on television is not one of them" (as quoted in the 2007 *New York Times* article "FCC Moves to Restrict TV Violence").

Use of V-chip technology in the home and external pressure on networks to rate their programs can be seen as an effort on the part of the government to control media content, and so First Amendment watchdogs are on the alert. Television is not the only medium the government has tried to restrict. The

In 2004, protesters at the Republican National Convention in New York City protest the policies of President George W. Bush, including the wars in Iraq and Afghanistan and the curtailment of civil liberties such as freedom of speech.

newest communications frontier—the Internet—is the subject of much debate regarding free speech rights.

FREE SPEECH FOR ALL!

Free speech is not just about saying what you want. It is also about listening to the music or words you want to listen to, reading books you freely choose and want to read, listening to (and then possibly choosing to ignore) opinions with which you disagree, and accepting or rejecting the meaning conveyed by other people's symbolic speech and acts. We were given this important freedom so that we might keep ourselves safe from the tyranny of a government with too much power, including the power to restrict knowledge, thought, information, action, ideas, and speech. No one voice should have authority over all other voices. It is important not only that we exercise this right, speaking out for what we believe, but that we also protect this right for others, in part by listening to those ideas and words we don't believe in, or at least allowing them to be freely expressed.

PREAMBLE TO THE CONSTITUTION

We the People of the United States, in order to form a more perfect Union, establish Justice, insure domestic Tranquility, provide for the common defense, promote the general Welfare, and secure the Blessings of Liberty to ourselves and our Posterity, do ordain and establish this Constitution for the United States of America.

On September 25, 1789, Congress transmitted to the state legislatures twelve proposed amendments, two of which, having to do with congressional representation and congressional pay, were not adopted. The remaining ten amendments became the Bill of Rights.

THE BILL OF RIGHTS

Amendment I

Congress shall make no law respecting an establishment of religion, or prohibiting the free exercise thereof; or abridging the freedom of speech, or of the press; or the right of the people peaceably to assemble, and to petition the Government for a redress of grievances.

Amendment II

A well regulated Militia, being necessary to the security of a free State, the right of the people to keep and bear Arms, shall not be infringed.

Amendment III

No Soldier shall, in time of peace be quartered in any house, without the consent of the Owner, nor in time of war, but in a manner to be prescribed by law.

Amendment IV

The right of the people to be secure in their persons, houses, papers, and effects, against unreasonable searches and seizures, shall not be violated, and no Warrants shall issue, but upon probable cause, supported by Oath or affirmation, and particularly describing the place to be searched, and the persons or things to be seized.

Amendment V

No person shall be held to answer for a capital, or otherwise infamous crime, unless on a presentment or indictment of a Grand Jury, except in cases arising in the land or naval forces, or in the Militia, when in actual service in time of War or public danger; nor

shall any person be subject for the same offence to be twice put in jeopardy of life or limb; nor shall be compelled in any criminal case to be a witness against himself, nor be deprived of life, liberty, or property, without due process of law; nor shall private property be taken for public use, without just compensation.

Amendment VI

In all criminal prosecutions, the accused shall enjoy the right to a speedy and public trial, by an impartial jury of the State and district wherein the crime shall have been committed, which district shall have been previously ascertained by law, and to be informed of the nature and cause of the accusation; to be confronted with the witnesses against him; to have compulsory process for obtaining witnesses in his favor, and to have the Assistance of Counsel for his defense.

Amendment VII

In Suits at common law, where the value in controversy shall exceed twenty dollars, the right of trial by jury shall be preserved, and no fact tried by a jury, shall be otherwise reexamined in any Court of the United States, than according to the rules of the common law.

Amendment VIII

Excessive bail shall not be required, nor excessive fines imposed, nor cruel and unusual punishments inflicted.

Amendment IX

The enumeration in the Constitution, of certain rights, shall not be construed to deny or disparage others retained by the people.

Amendment X

The powers not delegated to the United States by the Constitution, nor prohibited by it to the States, are reserved to the States respectively, or to the people.

GLOSSARY

amendment An addition or change to the U.S. Constitution.

anarchist A person who supports the idea that no one should be in control and that there should be no government.

boycott To refuse to buy something or take part in something as a way to protest.

censorship The practice of wholly or partially suppressing books, newspapers, scripts, etc., in order to protect the public from harmful, offensive, or dangerous material.

civil rights The rights that all members of a society have to freedom and equal treatment under the law.

Communist A person who supports the idea that all land, property, goods, and businesses in a country belong to the government or the community, and everyone shares the profits.

Congress The branch of the U.S. government that makes laws. It is made up of the Senate and the House of Representatives.

conservative Someone who opposes radical change and wants things to stay as they are or as they used to be.

constitution A document that establishes the fundamental laws of a state or a country.

Continental Congress The first organized government in America outside of British rule.

dissent Disagreement with an opinion or an idea.

fighting words Any words directed at a specific person that would start a fight and endanger others.

hierarchical A system of organizing people or units according to different ranks, with each rank having a different amount of power.

inalienable Incapable of being surrendered.

kaiser The official title of the German Emperor and King of Prussia Friedrich Wilhelm Victor Albert (1859–1941).

legislation Laws that have been proposed or passed.

liberal Someone who is in favor of political change and reform.

monopoly Complete control of something, such as a supply of a product.

obscenity A word or image that is shocking and indecent.

pacifist A person who believes that war and violence are wrong and refuses to fight.

prurient Lustful, lewd, or full of desire.

reason The ability to think rationally, using logic instead of emotion to arrive at a conclusion.

sedition The act of encouraging rebellion against authority with the aim of overturning a state.

segregation The practice of keeping people of different races apart.

Socialist A person who supports an economic system in which the government controls the production of goods by factories, businesses, and farms.

subjects People who live under the authority of a king or queen.

suffragette A female supporter of women's suffrage, or the right of women to vote. In the United States, women won the right to vote in 1920.

Supreme Court The highest and most powerful court in the United States. It can declare laws unconstitutional.

American Civil Liberties Union (ACLU)
125 Broad Street, 18th Floor
New York, NY 10004
(212) 549-2500
Web site: http://www.aclu.org
The ACLU views itself as the nation's guardian of liberty, working daily in courts, legislatures, and communities to defend and preserve the individual rights and liberties that the Constitution and laws of the United States guarantee everyone in this country. These rights include free speech, freedom of the press, freedom of association and assembly, freedom of religion, freedom from discrimination, the right to due process, and the right to privacy.

Center for Democracy and Technology (CDT)
1634 I Street NW, Suite 1100
Washington, DC 20006
(202) 637-9800
Web site: http://www.cdt.org
The CDT is a nonprofit public interest organization working to keep the Internet open, innovative, and free. As a civil liberties group with expertise in law, technology, and policy, the CDT works to enhance free expression and privacy in communications technologies by finding practical and innovative solutions to public policy challenges while protecting civil liberties.

First Amendment Center
555 Pennsylvania Avenue
Washington, DC 20001
(202) 292-6288
Web site: http://www.firstamendmentcenter.org

The First Amendment Center supports the First Amendment and builds understanding of its core freedoms through education, information, and entertainment. The center serves as a forum for the study and exploration of free expression issues, including freedom of speech, the press, and religion and the rights to assemble and to petition the government.

Foundation for Individual Rights in Education (FIRE)
601 Walnut Street, Suite 510
Philadelphia, PA 19106
(215)717-3473
Web site: http://www.thefire.org

The mission of FIRE is to defend and sustain individual rights at America's colleges and universities. These rights include freedom of speech, legal equality, due process, religious liberty, and sanctity of conscience. FIRE views these as the essential qualities of individual liberty and dignity. Its core mission is to protect the unprotected and to educate the public and communities of concerned Americans about the threats to these rights on American campuses and the means to preserve them.

The Freedom Forum
555 Pennsylvania Avenue NW
Washington, DC 20001
(202) 292-6100
Web site: http://www.freedomforum.org

The Freedom Forum, based in Washington, D.C., is a nonpartisan foundation that champions the First Amendment as a cornerstone of democracy. The Freedom Forum is the main funder of the operations of the Newseum in Washington, D.C., the First Amendment Center, and the Diversity Institute.

Freedom to Read Foundation

American Library Association
50 East Huron Street
Chicago, IL 60611
(800) 545-2433, ext. 4226
Web site: http://www.ftrf.org
The Freedom to Read Foundation was established in 1969 as a First Amendment legal defense organization affiliated with the American Library Association.

National Coalition Against Censorship (NCAC)

275 Seventh Avenue, #1504
New York, NY 10001
(212) 807-6222
Web site: http://www.ncac.org
The NCAC, founded in 1974, is an alliance of fifty national non-profit organizations, including literary, artistic, religious, educational, professional, labor, and civil liberties groups. United by a conviction that freedom of thought, inquiry, and expression is a fundamental human right and essential to a healthy democracy, the NCAC works to educate its members and the public at large about the dangers of censorship and how to oppose them.

People for the American Way

2000 M Street NE, Suite 400
Washington, DC 20036
(202) 467-4999
Web site: http://www.pfaw.org

People for the American Way is dedicated to making the promise of America real for every American, in part by working to ensure equality, freedom of speech, freedom of religion, the right to seek justice in a court of law, and the right to cast a vote that counts. Its mission is to promote and maintain a vibrantly diverse democratic society in which everyone is treated equally under the law, given the freedom and opportunity to pursue their dreams, and encouraged to participate in the nation's civic and political life. Its vision of America is of a nation and a people that respect diversity, nurture creativity, and combat hatred and bigotry.

Student Press Law Center

1101 Wilson Boulevard, Suite 1100

Arlington, VA 22209-2275

(703) 807-1904

Web site: http://www.splc.org

The Student Press Law Center seeks to improve the climate for student journalism in all forms by breaking down barriers that prevent students from gathering, publishing, or airing news and commentary; reducing censorship of students' journalistic work; educating students about their responsibilities as journalists; and improving students' access to essential documents and meetings and teaching them to put the knowledge gained to productive use.

Supreme Court of the United States

1 First Street NE

Washington, DC 20543

(202) 479-3000

Web site: http://www.supremecourt.gov

The Supreme Court of the United States is the highest judicial body in the United States and leads the federal judiciary.

It consists of the chief justice of the United States and eight associate justices who are nominated by the president and confirmed by a majority vote of the Senate. Once appointed, justices effectively have life tenure, which terminates only upon death, resignation, retirement, or conviction on impeachment. The Court meets in Washington, D.C., in the U.S. Supreme Court Building. The Supreme Court primarily hears appeals of lower court decisions.

WEB SITES

Due to the changing nature of Internet links, Rosen Publishing has developed an online list of Web sites related to the subject of this book. This site is updated regularly. Please use this link to access the list:

www.rosenlinks.com/pfcd/spee

Abrams, Floyd. *Speaking Freely: Trials of the First Amendment*. New York, NY: Penguin Books, 2006.

Amar, Vikram David, ed. *The First Amendment, Freedom of Speech: Its Constitutional History and the Contemporary Debate*. Amherst, NY: Prometheus Books, 2009.

Barron, Jerome A., and C. Thomas Dienes. *First Amendment in a Nutshell*. Eagan, MN: West, 2008.

Finan, Christopher M. *From the Palmer Raids to the PATRIOT Act: A History of the Fight for Free Speech in America*. Boston, MA: Beacon Press, 2008.

Fradin, Dennis Brindell. *The Bill of Rights* (Turning Points in U.S. History). Tarrytown, NY: Marshall Cavendish Children's Books, 2008.

Isaacs, Sally Senzell. *Understanding the Bill of Rights* (Documenting Early America). New York, NY: Crabtree Publishing Co., 2008.

Leavitt, Amie J. *The Bill of Rights in Translation: What It Really Means*. Mankato, MN: Capstone Press, 2008.

Lewis, Anthony. *Freedom for the Thought That We Hate: A Biography of the First Amendment*. New York, NY: Basic Books, 2010.

O'Brien, David M. *Congress Shall Make No Law: The First Amendment, Unprotected Expression, and the U.S. Supreme Court*. Rowman & Littlefield Publishers, Inc., 2010.

Shiffrin, Steven H. *First Amendment: Cases, Comments, Questions*. Eagan, MN: West, 2006.

Sobel, Syl. *The Bill of Rights: Protecting Our Freedom Then and Now*. Hauppauge, NY: Barron's Educational Series, 2008.

Stone, Geoffrey R. *Perilous Times: Free Speech in Wartime: From the Sedition Act of 1798 to the War on Terrorism*. New York, NY: W. W. Norton, 2005.

Sullivan, Kathleen M. *First Amendment Law*. 3rd ed. New York, NY: Foundation Press, 2007.

Sunstein, Cass R., et al. *The First Amendment*. 3rd ed. New York, NY: Aspen Publishers, Inc., 2008.

Taylor-Butler, Christine. *The Bill of Rights*. New York, NY: Children's Press, 2008.

Volokh, Eugene. *First Amendment and Related Statutes: Problems, Cases, and Policy Arguments*. New York, NY: Foundation Press, 2008.

Warburton, Nigel. *Free Speech: A Very Short Introduction*. New York, NY: Oxford University Press, 2009.

Wolfson, Nicholas. *Hate Speech, Sex Speech, Free Speech*. Westport, CT: Praeger, 2008.

Yero, Judith Lloyd. *American Documents: The Bill of Rights*. Des Moines, IA: National Geographic Children's Books, 2006.

ABOUT THE AUTHORS

Sally Ganchy is a writer who lives in New York City.

Claudia Isler is an editor and writer who has written numerous books, including ones on custody laws and voting rights. She lives in Pennsylvania.

PHOTO CREDITS

Cover, pp. 1, 10, 22, 30, 45, 66, 79, 98, 114, 126 Roll Call/ Getty Images; p. 4 NY Daily News via Getty Images; pp. 12, 32, 35, 84 Library of Congress Prints and Photographs Division; p. 14 © ClassicStock/Alamy; p. 18 Larry Downing/ Reuters/Landov; p. 25 Jim Watson/AFP/Getty Images; p. 28 Doug Kanter/AFP/Getty Images; pp. 39, 46, 71, 77, 100, 119 © AP Images; p. 43 Michael Springer/Getty Images; p. 49 Time & Life Pictures/Getty Images; p. 53 Dick Swanson/ Time & Life Pictures/Getty Images; pp. 63, 80 Linda Davidson/The Washington Post/Getty Images; p. 68 Michael Smith/Getty Images; p. 75 Justin Guariglia/National Geographic/Getty Images; p. 93 Hulton Archive/Getty Images; p. 96 © Grant T Morris/ZUMA Press; pp. 104–105 David McNew/Getty Images; p. 108 Paul J. Richards/AFP/ Getty Images; p. 111 Jemal Countess/WireImage/Getty Images; pp. 116–117 © Susan Tusa/Detroit Free Press/ ZUMA Press; p. 126 Nicholas Kamm/AFP/Getty Images; pp. 132–133 Scott J. Ferrell/Congressional Quarterly/Getty Images; Other Interior Images © www.istockphoto.com.

Photo Researcher: Amy Feinberg